T0318076

SEAN PALMER

SUZANNE STABILE, SERIES EDITOR

FORTY DAYS ON

BEING A THREE

ENNEAGRAM DAILY REFLECTIONS

An imprint of InterVarsity Press
Downers Grove, Illinois

To Rochelle

thank you for loving me.

◉ ◉ ◉ ◉

InterVarsity Press
P.O. Box 1400, Downers Grove, IL 60515-1426
ivpress.com
email@ivpress.com

InterVarsity Press® is the book-publishing division of InterVarsity Christian Fellowship/USA®, a movement of students and faculty active on campus at hundreds of universities, colleges, and schools of nursing in the United States of America, and a member movement of the International Fellowship of Evangelical Students. For information about local and regional activities, visit intervarsity.org.

All Scripture quotations, unless otherwise indicated, are taken from The Voice™. Copyright © 2008 by Ecclesia Bible Society. Used by permission. All rights reserved.

While any stories in this book are true, some names and identifying information may have been changed to protect the privacy of individuals.

Published in association with The Bindery Agency, www.thebinderyagency.com.

Enneagram figure by InterVarsity Press

Cover design and image composite: David Fassett
Interior design: Daniel van Loon
Images: gold foil background: © Katsumi Murouchi / Moment Collection / Getty Images
paper texture background: © Matthieu Tuffet / iStock / Getty Images Plus

ISBN 978-0-8308-4746-4 (print)
ISBN 978-0-8308-4747-1 (digital)

Printed in the United States of America ∞

InterVarsity Press is committed to ecological stewardship and to the conservation of natural resources in all our operations. This book was printed using sustainably sourced paper.

Library of Congress Cataloging-in-Publication Data
A catalog record for this book is available from the Library of Congress.

P 20 19 18 17 16 15 14 13 12 11 10 9 8 7 6 5 4 3 2 1
Y 37 36 35 34 33 32 31 30 29 28 27 26 25 24 23 22 21 20

WELCOME TO ENNEAGRAM DAILY REFLECTIONS

Suzanne Stabile

The Enneagram is about nine ways of seeing. The reflections in this series are written from each of those nine ways of seeing. You have a rare opportunity, while reading and thinking about the experiences shared by each author, to expand your understanding of how they see themselves and how they experience others.

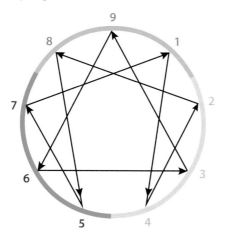

I've committed to teaching the Enneagram, in part, because I believe every person wants at least these two things: to belong, and to live a life that has meaning. And I'm sure that learning and working with the Enneagram has the potential to help all of us with both.

Belonging is complicated. We all want it, but few of us really understand it. The Enneagram identifies—with more accuracy than any other wisdom tool I know—why we can achieve belonging more easily with some people than with others. And it teaches us to find our place in situations and groups without having to displace someone else. (I'm actually convinced that it's the answer to world peace, but some have suggested that I could be exaggerating just a bit.)

If our lives are to have meaning beyond ourselves, we will have to develop the capacity to understand, value, and respect people who see the world differently than we do. We will have to learn to name our own gifts and identify our weaknesses, and the Enneagram reveals both at the same time.

The idea that we are all pretty much alike is shattered by the end of an introductory Enneagram workshop or after reading the last page of a good primer. But for those who are teachable and open to receiving Enneagram wisdom about each of the nine personality types, the shock is accompanied by a beautiful and unexpected gift: they find that they have more compassion for themselves and more grace for others and it's a guarantee.

The authors in this series, representing the nine Enneagram types, have used that compassion to move toward a greater understanding of themselves and others whose lives intersect with theirs in big and small ways. They write from experiences that reflect racial and cultural difference, and they have been influenced by different faith beliefs. In working with spiritual directors, therapists, and pastors they identified many of their own habits and fears, behaviors and motivations, gifts and challenges. And they courageously talked with those who are close to them about how they are seen and experienced in relationship.

As you begin reading, I think it will be helpful for you to be generous with yourself. Reflect on your own life—where you've been and where you're going. And I hope you will consider the difference between change and transformation. *Change* is when we take on something new. *Transformation* occurs when something old falls away, usually beyond our control. When we see a movie, read a book, or perhaps hear a sermon that we believe "changed our lives," it will seldom, if ever, become transformative. It's a good thing and we may have learned a valuable life lesson, but that's not transformation. Transformation occurs when you have an experience that changes the way you understand life and its mysteries.

When my Dad died, I immediately looked for the leather journal I had given to him years before with the request that he fill it with stories and things he wanted me to know. He had only written on one page:

Anything I have achieved or accomplished
in my life is because of the gift of your mother
as my wife. You should get to know her.

I thought I knew her, but I followed his advice, and it was one of the most transformative experiences of my life.

From a place of vulnerability and generosity, each author in this series invites us to walk with them for forty days on their journeys toward transformation. I hope you will not limit your reading to only your number. Read about your spouse or a friend. Consider reading about the type you suspect represents your parents or your siblings. You might even want to read about someone you have little affection for but are willing to try to understand.

You can never change *how* you see, but you can change what you *do* with how you see.

ON BEING A THREE

"Everyone needs a spiritual director *and* a therapist," says my friend Suzanne Stabile. So I spend Monday mornings with John.

John is my therapist, my "I don't give a crap who you are" guy. As an Enneagram Three, I find it helpful to know John and people like him—people who couldn't care less what I do, who I know, or what I've accomplished.

My first spiritual director was Don, who I met in seminary at Fuller Northern California. Don showed me what it looked like to be real, open, and honest. Before he knew me much at all, he shared with me his victories and defeats, as a son, husband, father, and businessman. He was open about the one thing I don't want to share with anyone, even myself: failure.

As an Enneagram Three, my core sin is deceit. That doesn't really mean what people often think it does. It doesn't mean I lie, though, at times, I'm confident I do. Deceit means I live at the edge of duplicity. I don't want to. I want to be esteemed. I want to be admired. I want to be loved. I want to be in relationship with people. In fact, I want to be in relationship with people more than I want anything else. But somewhere along my path I got the misguided idea that being loved required being valuable, worthwhile, or at least *looking* valuable and worthwhile. And not just successful in some generic or universal sense, but successful in presenting a version of myself that the person or the room of people before me wanted to see.

There's just no way to be successful at looking successful to everyone without creatively shading the picture. That's deceit.

In one of my favorite movies, *A Few Good Men*, Demi Moore's Lt. Cdr. JoAnne Galloway and Tom Cruise's Lt. Daniel Kaffee go out for seafood. After Galloway gives Kaffee a rundown of her accomplishments, Kaffee asks, "Why are you always giving me your résumé?" JoAnne responds, "Because I want you to think that I'm a good lawyer." I don't know where JoAnn Galloway might type herself on the Enneagram (I never, ever, ever type other people), but Galloway's response was pure Enneagram Three.

And that's why I need John and Don.

They don't care about my résumé. Giving it to them would make me feel silly, stupid even.

My problem is I've spent a good bit of time and energy building that résumé. I've been in professional ministry for over twenty-three years, currently serving as teaching pastor for a large church in Houston, Texas. I'm also a writer, speaker, and coach for other speakers and preachers. At the same time, I enjoy the gifts of a wonderful wife, Rochelle, and two beautiful teenaged daughters, Malia and Katharine. I have both a home office and a home gym because my daily instinct is to *do* something.

When I signed the contract for my first book, *Unarmed Empire: In Search of Beloved Community*, I called Don. All my other friends received the news with excitement. Not Don. There were no "congratulations." No "well done." No "you've earned it." Don said, "Wow! How do you think that will impact your relationships with Rochelle and your daughters?"

I felt deflated. Why? *Because I want you to think I'm a good . . . pastor.*

Like Don, John doesn't care if I'm a good pastor. He's more concerned if being a pastor is good for me. Every Enneagram Three needs both a John and a Don. We need people who don't care about what we've accomplished or are trying to accomplish. We need someone who looks at our failures with grace and kindness, who knows those false steps are passing realities of life and not a reflection of our value.

You might not have found a John or a Don yet. Even if you haven't discovered your "I don't give a crap who you are" people, you don't really need to in order to unearth the truth your heart needs most: you are loved.

Stop.

Dwell on that.

You are loved.

The best thing you can do right now is let your heart hunker down in the deep truth that you are loved and lovable. The late Catholic priest, writer, and theologian Henri Nouwen wrote,

> The world tells you many lies about who you are, and you simply have to be realistic enough to remind yourself of this. Every time you feel hurt, offended, or rejected, you have to dare to say to yourself: These feelings, strong as they may be, are not telling me the truth about myself. The truth, even though I cannot feel it right now, is that I am the chosen child of God, precious in God's eyes, called the Beloved from all eternity, and held safe in an everlasting belief.

And isn't love what you most deeply crave?

The Enneagram came to me after a series of prolonged and public failures, the kind that left me crying in bed at night and crushingly disappointed with God and myself. And I'm glad that it did. Had the Enneagram arrived any sooner, my outsized ego and dreams of a flourishing future would have silenced its wisdom. The beauty of failure—at least the beauty around *my* failures—was that in the midst of it, God revealed to me who my friends were, who my friends weren't, and who loved me for me, rather than for what I did or how I performed. In a world consumed with fans and followers, nothing can replace the abiding love of the faithful people God surrounds you with.

The beauty of the Enneagram is its dynamic nature. For starters, you are not your number. You are your true self, the beautiful, wonderfully made person you were created to be, your "essence," in Enneagram language. Your Enneagram number is a strategy to find love and meaning; that number is an explanation, not a reason or excuse for stagnancy or complacency. The Enneagram works best as a tool for growth, not a mechanism for a system of stasis.

Besides your core number, there are three crucial aspects of the Enneagram you will need to be aware of—your behavioral changes in stress and security, your "wings," and "subtypes."

First, let's consider the direction of the arrows, or what some Enneagram teachers call "integration/disintegration" or "stress/security." Stress and security seem more evocative and truer to my personal experience, so, with apologies to and with an appreciation for various schools of thought and experiences, I will use "stress/security" for shorthand throughout. In stress and security, each Enneagram type takes on some of the positive or negative behaviors of other types. For example, Enneagram Threes in security and integration adopt the positive or negative behaviors of Enneagram Sixes; while in stress, Threes will take on the positive or negative behaviors of Enneagram Nines.

There are three key distinctions we need to be aware of concerning stress and security. For one, no one "moves" to another number. Your core personality persists. We merely take on the behaviors and not the motivations of another number. Second, inside this dynamism you can adopt either (or both) the positive or negative behaviors of the other number. This is commonly called the "high" or "low" side of your stress and security numbers. Many Enneagram students misdiagnose their numbers because they examine their behaviors (not their motivations) only to find out, often much later, that they had actually been living in stress when they encountered the Enneagram and weren't who they thought they were. Third, the behaviors we adopt in stress and security are necessary to survive. For instance, there was a time I was frustrated by a coworker who consistently shut down my ideas, even those our organizations spent thousands of dollars creating. After a time I checked out—disintegrated to the low side of Nine—because it was either that or allow my frustration to grow to the point of lashing out or leaving my job. I knew I'd eventually re-collect and re-center myself, but for about six months, that Nine space and energy saved me. So you can see that the most important numbers to know besides your core number are your numbers in stress and security.

Second, you need to pay close attention to the numbers on either side of your core number. These are your "wings." Wings can be important or not, depending on your own spiritual journey and your location on that journey. It really is particular. Some of us, like me, have enormous wings, while others do not. The core of growth using the Enneagram will be found in knowing yourself within your number as deeply as you can.

Third, inside each core number are what Enneagram teachers refer to as instinctual variants, or "subtypes." The three subtypes are self-preserving, social, and sexual (also called one-to-one). Each person, in addition to having a core number, also lives from within their subtype. For instance, I am a self-preserving Enneagram Three while my friend Lisa is a social Enneagram Three. Her motivations come from her core number, but often people assume she's a Two because her subtype motivates her to curate successful social interactions for her and her family.

There is a widespread belief that subtypes are concretized and immoveable. That's not true. Thinking about subtypes, I'm reminded of a house my family lived in near downtown Houston. It was three stories. The entire house was ours, but at different times or seasons we spent more or less time on some floors. On the bottom floor was a garage and a guest bedroom with attached bathroom that doubled as my home office. The second floor contained our living room, dining room, kitchen, and a half bath, with two large bedrooms with en suite bathrooms. The laundry was on the third floor. When I was working on writing projects, I spent a great deal of time on the bottom floor, but none when my wife's second cousin moved in with us and we gave her that room. One summer when I could hardly sleep, I spent long hours in the living room on the couch. And when my wife or daughters had friends visit, I hid out in my bedroom. This is an apt metaphor for the same way an Enneagram

Three might be self-preserving at the height of her earning power and providing for a family, while a stay-at-home father or mother with young children might be social, only to have those subtypes change as life changes. Subtypes are not locked. Humans shift to these "floors" depending on what they need to do to survive.

However, stress and security, wings, and subtypes can be terribly fascinating but also incredibly distracting. Fascination is often a distraction from the hard work of transformation. The readings you are holding are aimed toward helping you find love and authenticity, not simply knowing more about the Enneagram. On one hand, finding love and authenticity means allowing God and the Scriptures to indict the deceit and vainglory that seeps inside and becomes a compulsive way of manipulating the world. On the other hand, these words attempt to harness the divine impulses inherent within Threes—our energy, focus, optimism, reflex for cheerleading, and so many other important virtues.

I suggest you read them slowly, reminding yourself that you, like everyone, are a mixed bag of virtues and vices. As a matter of fact, each of us can find ourselves in each of the numbers. Thus, this volume is not only for Threes. It's for everyone. So whether you want to explore a Three wing or to grow in relationship to a Three, you are welcome on this journey.

Our fugitive impulses, though resident within, are not our real selves. Some days these readings will make you angry. Other days you will feel affirmed. Still, there will be more days, if you are a Three, that you will feel nothing. And that's what I hope to change.

Every number on the Enneagram interprets the world through one of three centers—thinking, feeling, or doing—but is also repressed in one of those centers. For our purposes, let me explain it this way: though we receive the world through the heart and feelings, Threes don't use feelings to move forward, make decisions, or respond to the world. Threes are "feeling repressed" in terms of Enneagram wisdom. We are quick to do and think but not feel. That being the case, these readings will not ask you to do something each day; the readings are not task centered. Rather they will more often ask you to sit and try to raise your feelings, to make them intelligible and helpful to you. The only way for these readings to be rewarding is to show up for forty days.

Do the hard work. Read. Ponder. *Feel*.

Stop.

Dwell.

You are loved.

SHOWING OFF

KIM KARDASHIAN WAS ROBBED at gunpoint in a Paris hotel room in October 2016. The thieves strapped her to a bed, tied her arms and legs, and gagged her. When the men first burst into Kim's room they asked her about a specific diamond ring. It was worth $4 million.

A few days after the robbery, Kardashian said the robbers probably followed her entire Parisian trip. She posted her location and announced each party she was attending and what she was wearing on Instagram. She had even posted pictures of the ring they stole. Kardashian said they knew where she was and what she was doing because she was "showing off."

I like to think of myself as a deep, thoughtful, spiritual man but the truth is, I'm much more like Kim Kardashian than I am Joseph Kiwánuka. As an Enneagram Three, the bear on my back every day is the temptation to be seen. To be heard. To be considered. To be worthwhile. I'm a showoff in a show-off culture who gets rewarded for showing off. And the reward for showing off is more opportunities to show off. We call this "success," but as a friend of mine asked, "If a Three succeeds and no one is there to see it, did it really happen?"

And in my desire to show off, I disavow what the divine One says about me. When God promises me that I am fearfully and wonderfully made, that God will bring God's good work in me to completion, I reject it, vowing to wow the world on my own. In showing off, I disbelieve that I am seen, heard, considered, worthy, and more than that, *loved*.

Immersed and indoctrinated as we all are into a show-off culture but born with braggadocio, Threes too easily trade being admired for being adored by our Savior. I don't like to admit it, but I make daily attempts to get the world to look at me—whether through successes, physical fitness, or being considered clever or funny or smart or sophisticated.

What might today look like, then, if I were to simply pray the ancient words of the Jesus Prayer: "Lord Jesus Christ, Son of God, have mercy on me, a sinner!" Being healed means accepting the innate brokenness within us. Those broken places are the very things we are trying to hide by showing off.

In which area of your life are you most tempted to show off today?

What would it mean to enter that space and simply be present in your brokenness rather than in bragging about your "success"?

I CAN RUN FASTER
THAN YOU

I'M A COMPETITOR. It's encoded in the essential makeup of Threes. And anyone who has been around Threes knows it. I compete at everything, even when the person I'm competing with doesn't know (or care) that I'm competing with them.

In 2014 I lost one hundred pounds. That's when I discovered my love for running. The preceding year my doctor had told me that I was prediabetic with class 2 obesity. I didn't know there were classes to obesity, but I had reached the second one. I put my head down and got it done. First, I lost twenty pounds, then forty pounds, until I was down one hundred pounds in just over a year.

With my newfound love for running, I received my daughter's decision to also start running with great joy. Malia has never been particularly interested in sports, and we tried a few—softball, soccer, and finally, cross-country. When it comes to competition, she just doesn't thrive like I do. She just hops onto the field of play, content to win or lose.

So, when my daughter ran, my instinct for competition went into hyperdrive whereas hers did not. She ran for school credit and the endorphin release, not to win. I wanted her to compete so I could prove to the other parents, the coaches, and myself that I am a winner. It was a struggle to stand and watch her bring up the rear of the pack and then the rear of the rear. I did what I knew to do: cheer and congratulate. But what I wanted to do was slink away. I imagined the other parents seeing me as a loser. Her running made *me* feel like a failure. It made her feel alive.

When she runs, Malia feels pain, yes—but also freedom and release from her own desires for control. I had missed that in my craving for excellence. She had a different idea of excellent. And I'm learning that hers is better. St. Irenaeus said, "The glory of God is man fully alive." Running gave her life. Constant competition, even when I wasn't competing, depleted me of mine. I learned from Malia that the gift of the run is in the running.

Where can you release power today by refusing to compete?

How can you be vulnerable and open in this area?

Where can you allow the experience to be the gift to you rather than a pursuit to conquer?

LETTING YOURSELF LOSE

"THE EGO HATES LOSING, even to God," says Fr. Richard Rohr.

In the ancient world, the oldest brother received the largest share of the father's inheritance when the father died. Not only did the eldest brother receive the larger share, he also inherited leadership of the family and the judicial authority of his father. In Genesis 25, the eldest brother is Esau, but he received neither the responsibility of the family nor the larger share of his father's inheritance. Why? He was outwitted but his younger twin, Jacob.

After spending a long day hunting and coming up empty, Esau returned home famished. Jacob, who favored his mother and enjoyed staying near the house, had freshly made lentils. And as older brothers tend to, Esau demanded his little brother serve him, but Jacob had a different idea. He convinced Esau to abandon his birthright in exchange for the lentils. Jacob then tricked his blind, old father, Isaac, and made off with what wasn't his. By the rules of our culture, Jacob won.

Jacob is one of the patriarchs of Israel. He will always be honored. But his actions cost him something basic and human that seemed insignificant at the time: a relationship with his brother and separation from his mother. Jacob made a trade. In winning Esau's birthright, he lost his family.

Most Threes feel pressure to win at all cost, even though most of us don't have clear, undeniable moments when we trade our people for priority of place. It might be better for us if we did. Rather, we give away relationships little by little and piece by piece, in seemingly insignificant and inappreciable incidents—checking texts at dinner, returning email while "watching" our children dance or play sports, taking unnecessary business trips, expressing dissatisfaction when those around us fail to live up to our expectations, and many other daily attempts to win something that we have never even asked ourselves if it's worth winning.

The ego hates losing, but letting it lose might be the path to winning more of what matters.

Can you name what really matters to you?

What are the arenas of your life where you might be missing out on something crucial?

Take a moment and journal about what in your life you are truly unwilling to lose.

EMBRACING STILLNESS

PART OF MY MORNING ROUTINE is setting my intention for the day. I direct my energy and envision the most favorable outcomes for whatever I've planned. For all the wonderful results intentionality produces, the side effect is perpetual motion. My feet and my mind, like swift waters, are constantly running. Threes move fast and hard, hardly ever pausing to be in the moment, never being where they actually are.

Do you live in constant motion? Is your intention set on a million little things every day? If so, this may have served you well. You can see the tangible results of your efforts in your business and family. Sometimes it probably feels that if you were to slow down and take a break, the world wouldn't necessarily stop turning, but life might soon get out of control. So, you stay moving. But when you're always moving, you never discover the power of being still.

Think about that word.

Still.

When was the last time you were still? Not asleep. Not exhausted. Not binging Netflix to avoid the stressors of life, but truly and deliberately still. Movement is a means of distraction from the feelings and emotions that are always available and often undesirable.

What does stillness get us? Left behind. Overlooked. Passed over. Or at least we fear it will. But eventually a day comes when we feel used up and threadbare. All the constant motion gives the illusion of being alive and impacting the world, but the truth is, we've been spinning our tires in deepening mud. The engine is rumbling, but we're not going anywhere, even though all the shaking, rattling, and spitting dirt makes us think things are happening.

The signs that we're stuck are obvious—we're short-tempered with our kids; we continue carrying the emotional baggage loaded onto us by our parents; our sins become so routine that we abandon the notion that we might ever be set free. All the motion muffles the stirring of our souls, as if we're wearing soul-silencing headphones of the spiritual life.

As Jesus entered the desert before launching his public ministry, it's not remarkable that he endured forty days of fasting and praying. Plenty of people fast and pray. What is more Satan-defying is that he doesn't seem to accomplish much in the desert. He spends a lot of time being still.

What kind of deliverer starts deliverance by not delivering?

The space shuttle expends most of its fuel not in space but during liftoff. Before Jesus set out to preach, teach, and heal, he defies our expectations. He didn't speed up. Jesus slowed down.

The psalmist says, "Be still, and know that I am God" (Psalm 46:10 NIV).

When do we know that God is God? When we get still.

In our hurry, we unwittingly say, "I am God. If I don't get it all done, I'm defective. If I don't act, I will be abandoned. If I don't maneuver, I will be manipulated by others." Stillness teaches us a different rhythm. Stillness teaches us the good and beautiful work of God that asks for our participation but rejects our control. In stillness we allow our minds and hearts to quiet. In stillness we become self-aware. We notice all that we have sidestepped and hushed through our movement and noise.

Stillness forces us to engage deeper realities. There is no forward movement without stillness.

Embrace stillness. Get away somewhere without noise, absent of demands, and be still. Allow whatever happens to happen. If you get bored, fine. If you fall asleep, that's fine too. Just be still.

Allow stillness to anchor you to the present. Allow it to fasten you to the life you are living right now, to what is happening where you are. In stillness you learn to be fully present. And in the world and culture where we live, we could all use more of that.

TEARING DOWN
THE HOUSE?

HENRI NOUWEN WRITES, "For as long as you can remember, you have been a pleaser, depending on others to give you an identity. You need not look at that only in a negative way. You wanted to give your heart to others, and you did so quickly and easily. But now you are being asked to let go of all these self-made props and trust that God is enough for you. You must stop being a pleaser and reclaim your identity as a free self." There might not be more haunting words for Threes. Everyone is born with an essence—the essential, most spiritual, and most pure part of who they are. Our essence is our true self, the part that we express when healthy and the part of us that needs to be recovered—for a people-pleasing nature erodes a Three's essence.

Threes will do anything to be loved. But that's a pretty limiting way to live. People pleasing isn't simply done so more people will like us. Much of what we do is motivated by a desire not simply to be loved but to give love.

What could be more loving than to give people what they want? You work hard and contribute maximum effort at work. You provide for your family. You dream dreams for others that they lack the motivation and optimism to dream for themselves.

People have tried to tell Threes there's something wrong, something deceptive about looking out for the success of others while expanding their own capabilities—but what if there isn't? What if God made you the way you are for a glorious purpose? What if the drive to accomplish isn't something to dismiss but something to harness?

What if, right now, you are enough? My friend Brian Mann says, "Who you are is not up for negotiation." What if who you are is not under negotiation—but always renovation?

My wife and I bought a house in 2018. It was twenty-two years old, was dated, needed a serious facelift, and wasn't at all what we thought we wanted. We bought it because it was the right price, the right size, and in the right part of the city. It had good bones. We had to renovate! In a few months, we moved from kind of hating the house to kind of loving it. It took just a few changes for us to realize that a couple of renovations made life better. We came to love the house without needing to tear it down to the studs.

Likewise, who you are, your core, is inherently good and made in the image of God. You don't need to feel badly or apologize for the natural gifts that are inherent to who God created you to be. Spiritual formation is not about taking on a new persona; it's about releasing the false parts of that personality. The bones are good. You don't need to tear down your house.

> Take today and be present to the good that is already resident within you, remembering that you are fearfully and wonderfully made.
>
> Take a moment and read Psalm 8. Hear God's voice affirming the goodness of your design. Discover that God finds you completely pleasing.

PERFORMANCE VERSUS PREPARATION

the Oklahoma City Thunder in the Western Conference Finals. It was game six and the score was tied at the end of regulation. We were going into overtime. The Spurs' Tim Duncan was the best power-forward to ever play professional basketball, but by 2015 he had started on the downhill side of his career.

Russell Westbrook, the starting point guard for Oklahoma City, was a young highlight reel, all sizzle and spice. Westbrook also had a history of taking wild shots, and making questionable decisions at crucial times. The problem was that Westbrook was a point guard, meaning that he touched the ball every play. However, as a power-forward, Duncan only touched the ball when it was passed to him.

Though the game was tied at the end of regulation, the Spurs won by fifteen. Why? Every time the Spurs had the ball, they passed to Duncan in the low post. In overtime, Duncan was the only Spurs player to shoot the ball until they were up by ten points. Every time the Thunder had the ball, Russell Westbrook, a guard, playing farthest from the basket took the shot a lot. He missed a lot.

How does a player with declining talent beat a player in his physical prime?

Preparation. Threes are naturals at relying on performance rather than preparation. There are times when I believe that the force of my personality or natural insight or ability to connect with people will get me through. It's kind of a talent, and I bet the same is true for you. You've made it this far in life because you were able to produce at a high level, or at least make people think you were producing. But that will not always be enough.

I once heard philosopher Dallas Willard call the spiritual life "training for reigning." For Willard, preparation means immersion in spiritual disciplines: practices like silence, solitude, prayer, fasting, and secrecy. In time, these practices shape us into people who can be trusted to act rightly and kindly. Spiritual practices prepare our character so that we can more often avoid the pitfalls of performance.

Think through your days, weeks, and years to come—
the events, tasks, and interactions that await you.
Visualize the best outcomes from those activities and what kind of character is required to show up for your life.
Write those down. Pick one and dedicate your day to it.

KNOWING WHO
YOU ARE NOT

WHEN MY DAUGHTERS WERE BABIES, someone gave us a portrait book with pictures of babies dressed as adults. There was a baby in a suit, a baby in a fireman's outfit, a baby as a teacher, a baby as president. The suggestion was that these little babies could become anything they wanted to be, which is . . . not true.

When I was a college student, I spent a summer working in San Antonio, Texas. There was a local high school basketball player making big news. He was 7'1" and nearly 250 pounds of muscle. He had less than 3 percent body fat. After graduation, he was headed to play basketball at LSU. And whenever he left LSU, he was certain to be a star in the NBA. Everyone knew it. He was made for professional basketball. His name was Shaquille O'Neal. And Shaq did work hard to become an NBA Hall-of-Fame basketball player; but he didn't work hard to be 7'1".

At that time, I had more than 3 percent body fat and was only 6'1". My mother could have pored over those babies-as-adults books every day, but her baby boy was never gonna be Shaq.

I experience much more peace knowing the reality of who I am not. That's hard to hear for those of us who deeply believe we can shape the world to our desires. Yet you were born where you were born. You were born when you were born. You have the parents you have. You're wasting time if you are pushing back against natural realities about yourself that you didn't pick and you can't change.

Enneagram Threes spend a lot of time living into the lie that they can be anything, constantly shapeshifting. Simply because you cannot become *anything* you want does not mean that you cannot become *everything* you were meant to be. Coming to terms with what you cannot do opens you up to the beautiful possibilities God created for you.

What people or positions spark your jealousy or your spirit of competition?

What would happen if you examined your life and leaned into the roles and goals only you are uniquely able to do?

SETTING THE AGENDA

THREES LOVE TO SET THE AGENDA. More than just setting the agenda, we really dislike having someone else set the agenda. Threes wake up each morning knowing what they want to get done, what they need to get, and what others can do to make life run more smoothly.

Threes are laser-focused on agenda. We know the hurdles that have to be jumped on any given day, and we harbor a belief that if we think clearly and plan carefully, not only can we get it all done, but we can get it all done with excellence.

Our presence affects the world, we tell ourselves. And we tell ourselves this for a very good reason, because our presence so often *does* shape the world around us. We have a long track record of words said, ideas suggested, actions taken, paragraphs written, and goals met. And to be honest, we love this about ourselves. On the other hand, we are not equally in love with the idea that other people can affect us. Worse, we really dislike the idea that we need other people to make a deep and lasting impact on what matters most to us.

When you're the kind of person who influences the world it feels disempowering to *be* influenced. It feels limiting to need other people. The most we could possibly need, we think, is for others to stay out of our way or help us meet our agenda.

Three of the numbers on the Enneagram—Sevens, Eights, and Threes—form what's called the Aggressive (Assertive) Stance. Aggressive numbers are, well, aggressive. And that aggression is often helpful and productive. It can even be beautiful at times. At our best, this aggression means we can change the world for the better. But it also means we can sometimes run over people. We don't mean to. We aren't trying to. The fault here lies mostly with our pace.

I live in Houston, where on August 25, 2017, Hurricane Harvey devastated the city. Nearly four hundred thousand homes were destroyed, one of them being a rental property we owned. When we went to see the damage, what greeted our eyes was a four-foot-high water line along the drywall. The floors were ruined, the fences down, the house in shambles.

We missed the storm. We couldn't miss where the storm had been. That's how Aggressive numbers can be. We are often like storms with 156 mph wind speed, thrashing and moving things around, making an impact for sure. Our speed does damage, but we rarely notice the devastation we've left behind.

Have you ever expressly or subtly dismissed someone from your life the moment you realized they weren't going to be useful? Ever decided you were done with someone who couldn't keep your pace? Journal your response, or just sit with these questions and see what comes to the surface.

HOLY INTERRUPTIONS

IN JOHN 5, Jesus was heading to Jerusalem with his disciples for a festival. I imagine they were moving with some urgency, ready to party. Peter and James were talking, laughing, and making plans about who they wanted to see first. I envision them picking up their pace as they entered the portico of the Sheep Gate, each step drawing them closer and closer to the party. But all of a sudden, Jesus stopped. Right there next to the pool at Bethesda he saw a man lying there who had been an invalid for thirty-eight years, a man seemingly desperate for healing when the waters were stirred. Thousands of people had walked by him, them, too, in the rush of their own agendas.

But Jesus stopped.

Though they may have been in a hurry, the apostles found Jesus a few feet back, standing motionless beside a man lying on a mat. Jesus leaned over.

"Do you want to be made well?" he asked.

Jesus could have just healed the man and kept walking. No interruption. No stopping. But he didn't. He stopped. He lingered. He looked. He listened.

Have you ever handed a dollar or tossed change to someone begging without bothering to look them in the eye? Heck, that's doing a ton more than most people, right? This healing could have been as simple as Jesus looking at the man, lifting his finger, and signaling him to get up and walk. Healing could've come in a snap. Quick, clean, and efficient.

But that's not Jesus. Jesus stopped. Jesus delayed his plans. Jesus set his agenda aside.

When is the last time you stopped for someone? It certainly wasn't in traffic. It probably wasn't with your kids. How many times are you shouting at them, "Let's go! It's time to go." Stopping doesn't happen at work, either. "Is that project done? Report finished? We have to go!" Have you caught yourself asking someone, "How long is this gonna take?"

Jesus was open to interruption and found himself interrupted often—asked to heal or resurrect when those tasks were not on his agenda. And in the midst of those interruptions, Jesus doesn't respond like an average Enneagram Three would. He never became angered, miffed, or annoyed.

What is surprising to us is that Jesus accomplished a lot even though he was constantly interrupted. Jesus changed the world without a planner, an assistant, or time-management software. Perhaps there is an unseen productivity in our openness to interruption.

What might happen if you worked with your headphones off and your office door open? What might happen if you were open to people interrupting your agenda?

Perhaps you can take a step out. Find someone who just needs you to "stop beside the pool" and sit and talk with them.

HOLDING ON TO VAPOR

THERE ARE SOME LIES I'VE TOLD so often they have become truth, at least to me. I knew they were lies when I first told them. I knew they were lies when I trotted them out the second and third times, but somewhere along the way people believed them. And that allowed me to avoid having them ask me hard questions—and having told the same untruths, half-truths, and nontruths so many times, I saw those lies just settle in like a tire spinning in mud.

Average Enneagram Threes can be masters of deceit. We don't set out to deceive others, though in the end we do. We first deceive ourselves. Enneagram teachers Don Riso and Russ Hudson call our deceit what it is: vanity. I spend too much time staring into the mirror making sure that my shoes match my belt and my socks match my pants, but the vanity I experience is only momentarily connected to external concerns about my physical appearance and come more from a desire to connect with people by being what I intuit they want me to be.

The daily struggle of Threes isn't that we just want to look good. The daily struggle is that we shift, change, and adjust to look good for whatever audience we face, and that's an impossible task aimed at a slippery goal; it's like constantly grasping at a wet bar of soap. In one instance we need to look clever; in another, humble; in yet another setting, we want to appear well-read; and in another still, we want to look like we're down-to-earth.

According to the Hebrew Scriptures, King Solomon was astonishingly wealthy and wise. There was nothing available in his world that he did not possess or couldn't attain. Nearing his death, as he reflected on his royal life and accomplishments, what does he say about all his efforts?

"Vanity of vanities; all is vanity" (Ecclesiastes 1:2 KJV).

Before you quit your job, run up your credit card, or stick your head into an oven, "vanity" and "meaningless" might not mean what you think they mean. What he meant is that life is "vapor."

Vapor greets me every morning as I heat the water for my French press coffee. As I pour the water the steam rises. My wife, a science teacher, makes sure I know the steam is actually water—water *vapor*. Water vapor isn't meaningless or nothingness. It's real. It's there. I can see it. And if the water vapor is too hot and my face too close to it, it will burn me. What Solomon means is that vapor doesn't last. You can't grab it. You can't hold it. And for that reason, vapor is a great picture of deceit.

The person who wants to be clever, humble, well-read, and down-to-earth as they move from room to room can't possibly be a whole and seamless person. The people near us recognize the false front, but because mutating is so important to our sense of worth and value, and since Threes are so adept at it, we tell ourselves we've pulled it off. Oftentimes we do. But more often than we might think, we don't. All this deceit leaves us grieving the loss of our pure self, the self we give away by constantly shifting.

Today, treat vapor as what it is—elusive and impossible to hold. Look for ways you are shifting and maneuvering from one group to another. Try to hang on to one or two characteristics of your true self and carry that with you as the whole truth.

THE LITTLE WAY

AS A BOY, I WANTED TO BE Dale Murphy when I grew up. Dale Murphy played right field for the Atlanta Braves. He won the National League's Most Valuable Player in 1982 and 1983, when I was in second and then third grades. Murphy also won the Silver Slugger Award four years in a row, and the Gold Glove five years in a row. I wanted to bat fourth in the lineup, just like Dale Murphy. I wanted to wear number 3, just like Dale Murphy.

I thought there couldn't be anything better than being recognized and applauded, nothing better than having a stadium full of adoring fans, just as my childhood idol did. But the older I get, the more appreciation I have for the unheralded—someone more like St. Thérèse of Lisieux.

At the same age I was coveting baseball glory, Thérèse was dedicating her life to God. She knew from her earliest days she wanted to devote her life to the divine One. As a child, Thérèse spent most of her time being sick. She almost died, and Thérèse's mother died when Thérèse was four years old. Yet this early tragedy didn't stop Thérèse. After seasons of appeals, Thérèse was granted early entrance into the same cloistered convent with her older sisters.

Thérèse felt what many of us feel: she wanted to do great things for God, yet being cloistered meant that her options were limited. She wrote, "I feel within me other vocations. I feel the vocation of the WARRIOR, THE PRIEST, THE APOSTLE, THE DOCTOR, THE MARTYR . . . I feel the need and the desire of carrying out the most heroic deeds for You." Can you understand how she feels? Craving greatness while being pressed by life's limitations?

It wasn't long after giving voice to her disillusionments that Thérèse read St. Paul's encouragement to the Christians living in Corinth during the first century AD: "Each believer has received a gift that manifests the Spirit's *power and presence*" (1 Corinthians 12:7). When Thérèse read this, she went back to her journal: "I finally had rest . . . I understood that if the church has a body composed of different members . . . so I understood that the Church had a Heart and that this Heart is BURNING WITH LOVE . . . MY VOCATION IS LOVE."

Thérèse believed her job was to love, even at great sacrifice to herself. She decided that love meant taking the jobs inside the convent that no one wanted. She did the laundry and cleaned the kitchen, the bathrooms, and the messes of other people. She ate the leftovers and the food no one wanted. When Thérèse's older sister was made prioress of the convent just before Thérèse was supposed to leave her novice stage and become a full nun, because other nuns feared the politics of it all, Thérèse's sister asked her to stay a novice for life—which she did.

St. Thérèse pursued the opposite path of an average Enneagram Three. She released the dreams of being honored and sensational to be God's heart, to *be* love. Her approach to life is called *The Little Way* and has given life to the work of other world-changing leaders such as Dorothy Day and St. Teresa of Calcutta. These women changed the world through daily acts of love, which, in time, became great feats. They inspire me to seek small feats of great service rather than achievement.

Every day is an invitation to sacrifice your ego fixations and embrace God's heart of love. What unseen yet loving acts can you embrace today?

Ask for clarity about the sacrifices you can make to bring life to others.

WORTH REMEMBERING?

MY FATHER STARTED HIS CAREER in education as an American history teacher, and his teaching turned me into a fairly decent armchair historian. As a hobby, I've read biographies of almost every US president, but guess what? I can't name half of them without thinking about it really, really hard. Can you?

When I realized how quickly the most recognizable people can be forgotten, I decided to start paying attention to historical figures who might not get much airtime, like Simon of Cyrene from the Gospels. Simon was the bystander who helped the beaten, bloodied Jesus carry his cross up Golgotha. Simon quickly enters the story of Jesus and just as quickly exits. Three of the four Gospels remember Simon. Even at that, the Gospels don't quite know what to say about him. Matthew mentions him but quickly moves on. Mark calls Simon "a passerby," and launches into a conversation about Simon's kids, Rufus and Alexander. All Luke knows about Simon is that he's a man from the rural outskirts. It doesn't really matter which Gospel you read. Each says the same thing about Simon of Cyrene: not much.

Why did three of the four Gospel writers make a point to mention Simon of Cyrene but not mention all that much? Maybe because Simon teaches the beauty of anonymity. Simon isn't special. He does what anyone could have done. He's remembered for being the kind of person performing the kind of task most of us wouldn't remember.

When Matthew, Mark, and Luke remember Simon, they are slyly rebuking all our grand attempts to be memorable. Many of us spend too much time trying to be unforgettable or do something remarkable. We feel resentment creeping into our gut when our efforts go unnoticed.

Last week I was talking to John, my therapist, about a sermon a pastor and friend of mine preached. She was getting rave reviews from her church and online. It made me mad. I didn't think her sermon was great, not even good. I hemmed and hawed talking to John, and finally John said, "Sounds like you're jealous." Ouch!

He was right.

I was. But why?

I had to deal with the fact that somewhere inside I believe my life being meaningful is connected to my life being noticed, and for some reason I believe "noticed" is an endangered commodity with only so much to go around.

But all the presidents were noticed, yet very few are remembered. And Simon of Cyrene was hardly noticed, but remembered in Scripture for serving the Savior.

Embrace the simple service God puts in front of you—do the chores that aren't yours, allow others to merge in front of you in traffic, speak last in the meeting or don't speak at all, carry the groceries, unload the boxes, cover parts of the project that aren't yours—and don't expect any of it to be remembered.

SECRET-AGENT SPIRITUALITY

I'VE SPENT FAR TOO MANY HOURS architecting an online audience, what marketers call a "tribe." Once upon a time, blogs were popular. If you wanted to get noticed, get published, or be heard, publishing a blog was the way to do it. One year I dumped the cash my mother-in-law gave me for Christmas into all the blogging necessities to properly reach my awaiting tribe, readers who would turn me into a sought-after speaker and published author. Online pioneers before me charted a path that I could follow.

I followed all the rules: Post articles on certain days at certain times with certain keywords. Have the least annoying pop-up to encourage site visitors to leave their email addresses in exchange for a free resource. I learned to drive web traffic to my site by posting on every social media website in the universe and making sure each post had a way for readers to share with other potential readers. I became an expert sharer.

I had a vision for what I thought I wanted my life to be, and that meant I had to get noticed. And I did. The attention I sought, I got. Now I write books and crisscross the country speaking at conferences and churches. People introduce themselves to me and ask me to take pictures with them or sign their copies of my book. All that work, the 5:00 a.m. alarms, the networking, and the writing turned me into a blogging and social media machine.

It also turned me into an approval addict.

Early in life, Enneagram Threes become addicted to approval and its traveling companions, failure and success. Both failure and success are rooted not to an inner compass forcing us to reckon with ourselves and live out of an intrinsic righteousness, but in what we suspect other people will interpret as success. When we fail, especially when we fail publicly, we feel shame. That online platform I built, maybe like the successes you're trying to build, is tailor made for living and dying in another's gaze—either one of criticism or approval. My sense of self was measured by my perceived standing. For a long time, I just thought that was the way the world worked. But it's not.

Spiritually enlightened wisdom teachers have long shared a spiritual practice that cuts at our approval addiction. It's called *secrecy*. Secrecy is deliberately keeping our good deeds and personal virtues unknown. My wife calls it being a spiritual secret agent. Secrecy is crucial. It teaches me that God shapes my life and that whatever measure of influence

I've garnered wasn't simply the result of my efforts but was God's hand on my movements, and God's desire to use my voice. Secrecy allows me to live fully into God's purpose for my life without seeking stardom. It is possible, maybe if just every so often, to give your own public relations department the day off. Everyone doesn't need to see your latest workout or know what you're reading or writing, or where you're traveling or who you're with. Others don't really need to know about that speech you nailed, the deal you signed, the way you helped or changed someone's life, or whatever other achievement has lied to you by promising worth and significance.

How do you practice secrecy?

Do something good for someone and don't tell anyone. Don't post it. Don't take a picture for Instagram. Just do it and keep moving on. Then tomorrow do the same thing. And the next day, and the next day, and the next.

ROCKED BY AMADEUS

WILLIAM WILLIMON SAYS, "Envy works best at close range." Envy is one of the seven deadly sins, and it is always crawling right beneath the surface of our skin.

Enneagram Threes compete, and when I lean into my Four wing, my deeply felt desire to compete brings along his friend, envy. In a world where no one always wins, envy is only a second-place finish away. To be clear, envy is not ambition. Envy isn't really even jealousy. It's not greed or covetousness —not that those traits are good. Envy says, "I want what you have . . . and I don't want you to have it either."

In her book *Glittering Vices*, Rebecca DeYoung says that envy is at the heart of the movie *Amadeus*. As a boy, Composer Antonio Salieri prayed for musical talent and acclaim, pledging that he would give the glory to God. Salieri promised God both devotion and chastity in exchange for musical genius and fame. But when Mozart arrived on the scene, Salieri's dreams of greatness were dwindled in the shadow of Mozart's brilliance. How could God lavish such amazing gifts on such an arrogant, shallow buffoon as Mozart? Salieri wonders. Salieri becomes obsessed with Mozart, finally devising a scheme to kill him through exhaustion. That's envy: "I want what you have . . . and I don't want you to have it either." Perhaps the most villainous part of Salieri's plan was that while he was running Mozart into the ground, he also befriended him. Remember: "Envy works best at close range."

Envy shows up in feeling offended at others' talents and good fortune; it reveals itself in rivalries and shallow antagonisms; it shows its claws by celebrating other people's difficulties and distresses. When we're envious we read false motives into people's behaviors. We belittle and make false accusations. We talk behind people's backs, tell and retell gossip, and tease and bully and ridicule. Envy's trademark, it has been said, is wanting everyone else to be as unsuccessful as you are.

Envy is deadly because it kills the person God created us to be.

That was the case for Antonio Salieri, according to *Amadeus*, but it was also the case for Cain and Abel. God accepted Abel's sacrifice but rejected Cain's and told Cain about it. Abel had God's blessing, and Cain didn't want him to have it. Why didn't Cain repent and promise to do better next time? Why didn't he simply covenant with God to draw closer and rejoice at the opportunity for a second chance? Because envy turns our hearts away from others.

The Scriptures teach us to move toward others while envy moves us away from others. You can't "Love others in the same way you love yourself" (Mark 12:31) if you get bitter when your neighbor has it better. You can't "regard others as better than yourselves" (Philippians 2:3 NRSV) when regarding yourself first has always come first. There is no way to envy another and not deny the image of God in them. It's unlikely that envy will cause you to murder someone. But it will probably lead you to assassinate someone's character or diminish someone's reputation. The answer to envy, oddly, is not to stop envying but rather to "rejoice with those who rejoice" (Romans 12:15 NIV).

Are there people you envy? What could you do today to rejoice with them?

What might happen if, even when it feels awkward or strange, you rejoiced with and for others?

RETURN TO JOY

I'M STILL EMOTIONALLY RECOVERING from reading Paul Kalanithi's *When Breath Becomes Air*. Kalanithi spent nearly a decade training to become a neurosurgeon, but at thirty-six years old, he was diagnosed with stage IV lung cancer. As a child Kalanithi was fascinated by the reality that all organisms die. Since everything dies, he was haunted by a simple question: What makes a virtuous and meaningful life?

While being treated for cancer, Paul's wife got pregnant and gave birth to their daughter, shortly before he died in 2015. Near death, he wrote to his eight-month-old daughter:

There is perhaps only one thing to say to this infant, who is all future, overlapping briefly with me, whose life, barring the improbable, is all but past.

The message is simple:

When you come to one of the many moments in life where you must give an account of yourself, provide a ledger of what you have been, and done, and meant to the world, do not, I pray, discount that you filled a dying man's days with a sated joy, a joy unknown to me in all my prior years, a joy that does not hunger for more and more but rests, satisfied. In this time, right now, that is an enormous thing.

A joy that does not hunger for more. How profound, beautiful, and full.

Christians in Western, democratic, and consumer-driven cultures have almost no tools to deal with our hunger for more. We hunger for more income, hunger for more recognition, hunger for someone to see and fill the needs we can hardly name. For many of us, life itself has become about a kind of striving. And here comes Paul Kalanithani, a dying father, unburdening his infant daughter from a life of hungering. Her short life brought joy to a man with a shortened life.

I've always struggled to understand joy. Joy seems slippery and emotional. When Kalanithi writes about the joy his daughter brought him, it's not emotion though. What he means by joy is a state of the heart, an orientation of the soul toward another being.

Joy—more than a feeling or sapless sentimentality—is a pervasive sense of well-being. Our joy-filled moments are those when our lives are made whole, not in spite of the pains and sacrifices we've faced but because of them. Moments of "sated joy" are always connected to others. Joy is what we find not on the front side of delight but on the far side of pain: The joyful moments of parents seeing their children graduate or marry well after all the late nights, broken rules, and sacrifices made. The joy of a fiftieth anniversary celebration and when babies are delivered after hours of labor. Perhaps there is no joy without pain? Maybe pain is a precondition?

After a lifetime of striving for success and accomplishment, Kalanithi discovered meaning not in success or notability but through pain. Knowing that his days were few, the long hours of infant care that become burdensome to new parents became for him the spring of bliss. It's hard to imagine that Jesus—with all the meaning and beauty of the crucifixion—endured the cross for the sake of joy. But he did. There are some kinds of joy that can only happen through pain, a revelation that can only be seen once our eyes and lives have adjusted to a certain persistent darkness.

Today is not about embracing or enjoying suffering. No sane person signs up for that. Perhaps today, though, you can allow joy to mold you. What has God given you that brings you back to joy?

PARTNERS AND PROJECTS

IN TRADITIONAL ENNEAGRAM TEACHING, Threes are "Aggressive." But I like to think of us as assertive rather than aggressive. Aggression is often threatening or hostile. That's neither me nor many other Threes I know. I am, however, assertive in the way I meet the world. Assertiveness means tackling tasks and projects, waking up believing that the world can be shaped and that you have a role in shaping it. That also means that when something needs to be done, we're the ones to call. We get up and go—which can also be a problem.

A couple of years ago our family moved from one part of Houston to another. I took on the task with assertiveness. As our time to move drew closer, I handled all the details—rushing earnest money to the bank, finding a home inspector, and hunting down affordable movers. I did all this in one night. In fact, I did it all in a couple of hours one night, while my wife was sleeping.

She woke up displeased. She should've been consulted, she argued. We should've walked every step together, but because I'm me, we didn't.

There is a harm caused by aggressive personalities, because we tend to move quickly and alone. And the instinct to go it alone creates isolation.

What Threes need to learn is partnership. We can look to the apostle Paul for an example. I suspect Paul learned the importance of partnerships the hard way. In his early days of ministry, Paul's partner was Barnabas. In Acts 15, the two decide to revisit all the churches they'd planted, and Barnabas wanted to have another missionary, John Mark, hitch a ride. Paul said no. John Mark had deserted Paul and Barabbas on an earlier trip, and Paul figured John Mark was unreliable. In the end, the disagreement over John Mark was so severe that it cost Paul his partnership with Barnabas.

Could it be that Paul focused on the mission to the exclusion of John Mark? Paul was aggressive *before* he met Jesus on the road to Damascus. Paul was aggressive *after* he met Jesus on the road to Damascus. His focus changed but his personality didn't.

Do you worry that you've been Paul to someone else's John Mark, so focused on what needs to happen that people are left behind? The Scriptures don't say much about John Mark. He was there, he left, and he came back. Barnabas seemed excited to have him back while Paul seemed annoyed.

In the end, Paul went one way while Barnabas and John Mark went another.

Barnabas and John Mark went together.

Paul went alone.

And because of this, Paul never forgot the pivotal role of partnerships. Neither should we. Paul's life becomes marked by partnership, with friends like Timothy. And what does he call the women and men who share his worldview, like in Philippians 1? Partners.

In what ways are you using all your natural energy to push forward, which may be leaving others behind? Take inventory of this. Make a list of all the people God has brought into your life and how and why you need them.

Before you do anything else today, name your need for partners. The answer for the times when you are overly aggressive isn't passivity. It's knowing that you actually do need people.

NOT #WINNING

I GOT FIRED ONCE. Well, twice. The first time was in college when I worked at a bowling alley. The second was much later, much more public, and more costly. When the second firing came, I had a wife, two children, and no emotional resources to keep me from spiraling into despondency. I felt like a failure. In the course of my life I had come to believe that I was loved because of what I did. And when people who know you and have lived alongside you quit you, with the way I had come to see the world, what else could I have felt?

For typical Enneagram Threes, doing things successfully becomes the way we learned to get what we needed. Perform, achieve, win, succeed, and get it all done and you will be loved, praised, admired, and included. Isn't this what we all want? To be loved and accepted, to be admired and to belong. These are our deepest human needs. The problem with seeking these needs through being successful in our tasks is that failure is a part of life—and not just a part of life in seasons, episodes, or occasions. Failure is a daily part of life.

What would happen if we accepted failure as the daily reality it is? What if we stopped numbing ourselves to our failure and adopted Jesus' version of success?

Jesus reevaluates what we call "success." Consider what Jesus says when he describes the good life, often called The Beatitudes.

Words like *persecuted, meek,* and *poor* don't conjure up images of success in our culture. They didn't in Jesus' culture either. I fight the urge to quickly substitute words like *overcomer* and *conqueror* and *powerful* for *meek* and *persecuted* when I think about a picture of God's kingdom. But that doesn't seem to be the way of Jesus. Jesus led by serving and conquered by dying. There is the upside-down nature of success in God's kingdom.

What would it look like to view our own success with Jesus' lens? Maybe Jesus would remind you that how you define success is not the only way. Maybe Jesus would help you see your home and your children and your unpolished and unfinished work projects as gifts to be celebrated instead of problems to be fixed. Perhaps with the eyes of Jesus, you would view the tasks that you didn't accomplish as things that can wait and opportunities for tomorrow. Maybe Jesus would show you that your children, although perhaps disobedient, are clothed and fed and have a roof over their heads because of God's grace more than your effort. Can you listen to Jesus affirming you, with love and gratitude? Perhaps Jesus looks at the laundry or the crumbs on the floor and gently shows you that there is beauty in the messiness of life.

When we experience our own failure, we can embrace the poverty of spirit, the mourning that it brings, the purity of heart it develops in us, and receive it all as a blessing. In this, we can begin to more faithfully inhabit the kingdom of God in our midst. The next time you want to curl up in a ball and pull the covers over your heard, try remembering that success is not on Jesus' list of what describes the good life.

What if, in daily moments of failure, we confessed to Jesus, *I see this as failure, but I know my vision is blurred through personality and culture and the time and space that I occupy. So, tell me, how do you see this?*

ALL MARKETERS
ARE LIARS

ON A LONG DRIVE through a dark night, I was listening to a fellow Three being interviewed on a podcast. An awful thought hit me: *Listening to Threes talk must be an act of patience and perseverance for the people who work and live with us.* It even makes my skin crawl sometimes. When we're not careful, in just a few short minutes our conversation partners know what we do for a living, what we've accomplished as professionals, the size of our homes, and how much something we bought or earned cost. And that's on our good days. When we feel that we're lagging or falling behind, our speech is peppered with a constant reframing, or dare I say, outright lying. It all boils down to self-promotion.

Threes are great self-promoters. Self-promotion is a reflex of ours. And given our contemporary culture, self-promotion never seems awkward. How would people know to call us when they need a writer, speaker, attorney, teacher, singer, or whatever we do without a little marketing? How else will people be impressed with our laurels if we rest on them? It's hard to get a promotion without a little *self-*promotion, right?

I ask myself this when I launch into a recitation of my most recent accomplishments: Why do I want them to know this? The answer: worth.

In seventh grade a girl named Jessica told me the reason I wasn't invited to another classmate's birthday party when most of the class had been invited: "You ain't nobody." Threes find our worth in the praise of others, their esteem. We want to be invited to the party. Our strategy for finding that worth is "adding value" or performing well. When we aren't it's almost like we shouldn't be alive. The times I feel most worthless, I'm tempted to remind people of my worth. Why else would they have me around? I don't want to be a "nobody."

Do you remember when you decided that you weren't going to be a "nobody"? What Threes want more than anything is what everyone wants, to be loved. That's how we know we're not "nobody." Enneagram Threes believe we will be rewarded with love if we successfully become whatever the people in front of us want us to be for them. We think we'll be valuable. And to be worth something, we have to communicate just how much we're worth. Others need to know what's in our knapsack of accomplishments. And we think the only way for people to know about our knapsack is if we tell them.

In those moments, the moments I feel most tempted to cart out my achievements, I'm often called back to the apostle Paul—a man who changed the world and had more to promote than I could ever dream—who said, "The one who boasts must boast in the Lord" (2 Corinthians 10:17).

Today, when tempted to promote yourself, pray, *God's been very good to me,* because God has been good to you. And that's the only boast that can give you worth.

GO BIG OR GO HOME?

AS A PASTOR my least favorite question is "How big is your church?"

"Does it matter?" I want to respond. And why would it? Regardless of what televangelists do, my life is filled with the everyday duties of a typical pastor. I dedicate babies, perform wedding ceremonies, offer eulogies, walk with people through both the joy-filled and difficult times of their lives. I preach sermons. I cry. I laugh. I teach. I study. "How big is your church?" is a strange question. When someone tells me they're a schoolteacher, I don't ask about their class size. Accountants don't get queried about the numerical values of their various accounts. Professional athletes don't even get asked about their win/loss record, so the question about church size bugs me. The reason, though, doesn't have anything to with teachers, accountants, or athletes; it has to do with me.

For most of my ministry I've pastored churches of fewer than 150 people. I would hop on planes, travel to conferences, and meet with other pastors and be asked about the bigness of my work, and when I said "One hundred and fifty," it often felt like the air dissipated. The immediate sense given to me was that I wasn't very important and I wasn't very good. For years, there was nothing that made me feel more Lilliputian than "How big is your church?" Even worse than being asked the question, I found myself asking it more and more. Why wasn't my church bigger? Why wasn't I important?

And then one day I stopped. I stopped asking the question and answering the question. I had fallen into what Henri Nouwen called "The Five Lies of Identity": I am what I have; I am what I do; I am what other people say or think about me; I am nothing more than my worst moment; and, I am nothing less than my best moment.

Asking about my church's size or growth or budget felt like being defined by what I have and do and what people say or think about me. Those all seemed like legitimate metrics because if I truly was better or smarter or more capable, more than 150 people would want to jump onboard. Add to that the quote hanging in my office, commonly attributed to Walt Disney: "Whatever you do, do it well. Do it so well that when people see you do it, they will want to come back and see you do it again, and they will want to bring others and show them how well you do what you do." But few people were coming to church again, and no one was bringing their friends. All the widely recognized markers of competence were moving in the opposite direction of where I wanted them to go. If I choose to believe the lies of identity, then I'd also have to believe I am not beloved.

When I feel the tug of these five lies, I return to what Nouwen wrote about them: "We are not what we do, we are not what we have, we are not what others think of us. Coming home is claiming the truth. I am the beloved child of a loving creator."

> A mantra for today: "I am the beloved child of a loving creator." ("I am the beloved child of a loving creator" is my favorite response when I'm asked the most annoying questions.) Train yourself to say those words today and every day.

BELOVED

EVER WATCHED PARENTS interact with their newborn? Grandparents, aunts, uncles, even friends of the family have an absolute fit over newborn babies. They "ooh" and "ahh" and "coo" and laugh and give all of their attention to this tiny baby as if it is the greatest creature ever. Can't you hear them?

"Look at her. She just smiled!"

"Oh, he's drooling. You're missing it! Look! Look! Look!"

New parents will spend hours just staring at their new baby in utter amazement. And here is the most astounding thing about it. The newborn baby doesn't even do anything impressive. Babies are the object of adoration, praise, and love, and all they do is eat, sleep, and get their diapers changed. They don't tell funny jokes. They don't help around the house. They don't accomplish anything.

I loved my children from the moment they were born. Why? Because they were mine. They were a part of me. Before they did anything, they were loved.

This is significant for Threes because somewhere after infancy, the opposite message was reinforced. We learned we were loved for what we did and not for being. This can lead us to living in excess in our number, where we become overly achievement-focused, self-absorbed, and narcissistic, all in a quest for love.

All four Gospel writers record the baptism of Jesus. All four writers want their readers to hear what God says to Jesus at his baptism—that he is beloved. God spoke these words before Jesus did anything. Before he healed anyone. Before anyone was raised from the dead. As far as we know, Jesus had not preached a sermon or performed a miracle. Before Jesus was admired by anyone on earth, he was affirmed by God.

What would shift in your life if you were utterly convinced that God loved you, admired you, and affirmed you for who you are? What if you knew, deep down, that you will be loved by God regardless of the ways in which you succeed and fail? The truth is that God will never love you any more or any less than right now. What I know about myself and others I've pastored is that most people have little doubt about God's love. We doubt God loves us. There is a special category of people God loves, we falsely believe, and that category is everyone else. We think—and may have been told—that there are hoops to jump through or steps to take before God will love us. And it is the biggest lie in the world. Right now, just as you are, you are completely loved. Like a newborn, you are adored. You are God's child.

Read Matthew 3:13-17 aloud. Picture yourself going into the water alongside Jesus to be baptized. Imaginatively consider what you see. What do you feel? What do you hear? What do you smell? Imagine hearing the words from God about you: "This is my son/daughter, whom I love; . . . with him/her I am well pleased."

ENTERING INTO SILENCE

GOD IS. The Genesis writer tells us that in the beginning, before anything was created, God existed. God has always been.

What was God doing before we came along?

Genesis says, "The Spirit of God was hovering over the face of the waters" (Genesis 1:2 ESV). Not only that, but God already existed in community with Jesus and the Holy Spirit. Then God creates by saying, "Now let Us conceive *a new creation*—humanity—*made* in Our image, *fashioned* according to Our likeness" (Genesis 1:26). God was existing in community before creation began, and then we were created in the image of the Triune God as beings. God was doing more than just resting. God was being. And since we are created in the divine image, as spiritual teachers like the Dalai Lama and Fr. Richard Rohr remind us, "We are human beings, not human doings." So what if we practiced being and not doing?

Being silent. Being present. Being content. Being with others.

This could look like taking a vacation and leaving your laptop at home. Or ignoring social media. It could mean turning off the music or podcast on the way to work and sitting in silence. The proclamation that we are human beings and not human doings is a reality that sets us free from the pressures of productivity.

Believing we are human beings and not human doings is not intuitive, nor does it seem worthwhile. But this is where growth occurs. We have to practice being and not doing. We push forward until we achieve our goals and then maybe, just maybe, we will reward ourselves with a night off or a short vacation. We fight to disconnect from our phones or projects when our children are around (for example, I'm writing this while watching a movie with my daughters). All the while, we are missing something, the centering essential for our souls.

Very few spiritual practices connect us to the invitation to be and not do better than silence. Start with ten minutes, and set a timer so you are not looking at a clock or checking your phone. As you come to silence, bring your attention to your body. What is going on here? Check in from the top of your head to the bottom of your toes and notice anywhere that you are feeling tension or pain. Bring your attention to these areas and focus on moving your breath to them. As you bring your attention to your breath, try and allow a deep inhale to match your exhale. See if you can breathe in for ten seconds, allowing your lungs to fill completely with air, and then out for ten seconds, feeling your lungs retract. Do this for the entirety of your practice, taking slow and intentional breaths. If this is all you do for ten minutes, you will have succeeded.

Try this breath prayer. Breathe in, saying "Be."
Breathing out, saying "Loved." As you breathe in, you can receive the invitation from God to simply be, and as you breathe out, you can live from love.

LETTING IT BE

"YOU'LL HAVE TO BE twice as good to get half the credit," was my dad's most consistent piece of advice to me as a boy. His words embedded themselves in my heart because his wisdom was hard won. He was a child of the 1950s, a black man raised in Mississippi who earned a doctorate and spent his life in education. He had to scrap for nearly everything and didn't want that battling spirit to bypass his son. Dad taught me that if I wanted something, I was going to have to go get it. I couldn't count on anyone else to make my life happen. I appreciate his advice. In many ways it made me who I am. And that is both good and bad.

I'm not the only child who grew up with parents and authority figures who made sure we came into the world wearing a heavy coat of striving. They loved us enough to make sure we knew that life was going to offer toilsome, tiring times and to ride them out we would need to meet toil with grit. They were advocates for our ambition, and our lives would be less without them. But soon enough, we find that, if we are open to wisdom and the prompting of God, unhealthy ambition chokes out healthy vigor and may diminish more grand designs God has prepared for us.

For years I never understood why athletes who lost a game because of a teammate's blunder or lack of skill would say, "It is what it is." Turns out "it is what it is" is a strategy taught by sports phycologists who have to train athletes to accept what is not under their control. In life, sometimes the outcomes we get are not the outcomes we want, and that's okay. Humans are not gods. We can only do what we can do. No more. And to live into that reality requires surrender. Jesus says, "Unless you change and become like little children, you will never enter the kingdom of heaven" (Matthew 18:3). Imagine the kingdom of heaven to be a place where all things are right. And to enter into it, you must become like a little child.

"Let go and let God" is a threadbare cliché, for sure. But every so often it serves us well to trust God to deliver on God's promises, believing that we don't always have to do it all ourselves. Not only do we not have to be "good," we also don't need to get the "credit."

Is there something big on your agenda today? This week? Pause now and identify which aspects you can completely release. Write these down and let others connected to that project or proposal know that you will not fix or intervene in this one aspect of the plan. Then see what God does.

PACKING UP

I TRAVEL A LOT, which means I pack a lot. I love being in new places and meeting new people, but I hate everything it takes to get there. I am a TSA PreCheck passenger and avail myself of whatever premier or elite access I can beg, borrow, or steal. I am a lover of quick and efficient processes, including packing. I have a carefully crafted packing system. I've spent years studying packing. Yes, years. But I still hate packing.

Packing creates panic in me. I'm weighed down with worry that I won't have just the right clothes for every conceivable occasion. Once, when emceeing a three-day conference, I packed seven days' worth of clothes, complete with seven different jackets with matching belts, socks, and shoes. The other emcee wore a black shirt and jeans. Every day. Still, each morning, I'd get dressed, after a lengthy workout of course, take a picture of myself in the mirror, and fire it off to my wife with the question, "Does this look okay?"

I know. It's ridiculous. I'm shocked she hasn't left me.

Once, in an effort to reveal how insufferable I'd become,

my wife bought me a bathmat that read: "You look awesome!" Through the years I've tried to explain to her how my concern about image really isn't about having a great image for image's sake or even about me making a favorable impression. It's because I want to honor people I am with by putting my best foot forward. I want to honor them by honoring what they honor. That explanation is partly true, which means it's also partly false.

To live more honestly concerning my image, I've started to think differently about packing and getting dressed. I started giving myself thirty minutes—and only thirty minutes—to get dressed, from beginning to end. No more. No less. That means no wardrobe changes, no mix and match, much less any adjustment or image management. I also only give myself thirty minutes to pack for trips. I pledge to pack no more than three pair of shoes, though I'm still promiscuous about jackets. I join those practices with a daily prayer: "God, help me see me the way you see me." I'd like to have a more evocative and eloquent prayer at my disposal, but this is all I've got.

While Genesis proclaims that humans are made in the image of God, what the image conscious need to hear is apostle Paul's encouragement that we are being transformed from one degree of glory to another. This is how God sees me, as moving from one degree of glory to another, not from looking awful to looking awesome. How tragic it would be to trade increasing glory for fleeting beauty.

Perhaps the next time you are greeted in the mirror by the suggestion that you should look and appear a certain way and somehow be more handsome, more attractive, less of this or more of that, you will know that God's desire is for you to gain glory.

Today, whenever you pass by a mirror or catch your reflection, try this prayer: *God, help me see me the way you see me.*

STRESS RELIEF

"STRESS IS FOR OTHER PEOPLE." When Jed Bartlet uttered those words on *The West Wing*, everything in my spirit yelled, "Yes! Stress is for other people, not people like me." Not for people who believe their thoughts and actions can and do have an effect and who don't know what it is to not make and execute a plan. As long as there's a plan, there should be no stress. I've always thought that. Until the summer of 2017 when I, like TV's Jed Bartlet, couldn't sleep.

I never had trouble falling asleep. I had trouble *staying* asleep.

I was also grinding my teeth. All signs of stress, I suppose.

Stress comes as a surprise to me. I can't identify it and hardly know what to do when I recognize it. If it weren't for outward symptoms—sleepless night and grinding teeth—I wouldn't be able to spot when I'm feeling the strain and weight of life. I'd just keep pressing forward, assuring myself that "lesser people" had somehow been able to manage their lives, and if I am who I think I am, I ought to be able to do the same. Stress is for *other* people, and by "other," I suspect I meant "inferior." And I am wrong.

Every number on the Enneagram does the same thing when we feel stress. First we double down, going deeper into both the blessings and challenges of our number. For Threes that means acting less like we're stressed and doing more of what got us stressed in the first place. It took me a long while to learn that the same thinking that got me into a situation couldn't get me out of it. I couldn't solve problems my personality created—working too much, seeking approval and applause, financial security, or whatever else it was at the moment—by throwing more personality on top of it. I was covering myself in my own grave.

When I healthily deal with stress, however, I can lose the façade that I don't experience stress or am somehow above it. In that space, I learn to relax and unwind. I can let my competitive energy stand down. I see this often in my work, where I trust and respect my coworkers so greatly that my competitive juices seem to wane and I celebrate others' contributions and giftedness.

So many people and cultures around the world know and appreciate the value of releasing stress. Massages make me more tense, but my wife enjoys them. Mental health days seem to me like ways to simply pile up more work for later, but friends of mine find them absolutely necessary. Nonetheless, it's wise to have ways to de-stress.

When our family lived along the Texas-Mexico border in McAllen, Texas, the Mexican-Americans I knew there had what I then thought was an awful, frustrating saying: "Mañana."

"Mañana" didn't have anything to do with being lazy, as

some would like to characterize it. Rather it was firmly grounded in caring for one's whole self, a tradition of self-care, and weighing things appropriately. These friends of mine in this community had learned to push back on the life-distorting belief that human beings are limitless doers, that everything is urgent. It was a skill I desperately needed.

An entire culture created a hedge against self-made and other-demanded anxiety. Along the border I found connected families, a celebratory people, and a rich spiritual culture. It was there I learned that there are demands—maybe most demands—that can wait. These sisters and brothers were just better at life than I was. They were right. I was wrong.

> In stress, your reflex might be to embellish your accomplishments or seek attention. Those are not healthy options. Stress can alternatively be an invitation to sharing your pains by opening yourself to others. Release stress—even if you refuse to admit you have it—by giving up one responsibility today. Hand it over. Give it to mañana.

A PREFERRED FUTURE

AT 6:00 A.M. ON AN ordinary Friday my mom said, "Your dad and I are going to get a divorce this morning."

Thursday night I'd gone to bed with Friday's biggest anxiety being an Algebra test, for which I was woefully unprepared. That Friday, though, I became a stereotype—another black kid raised by a single mother. It's a picture I'm not fond of, a truth I don't like.

My parents divorced when I was fifteen. It was the early 1990s, and even though divorce was no longer the cultural shock it historically had been, most of my friends' parents were still married, and my parents' divorce came as a shock to me. Or perhaps I wanted to be shocked.

I thought about my story when my friend Sam sat with me at a coffee shop telling me that he and his wife, Melanie, were divorcing. Sam and Melanie had three sons who they dearly loved, but, like many couples under the sun-scorching heat of divorce papers, the two of them were prepared to go to war against each other. Alimony, custody, vengeance. Sam, trying to honor his wife for the sake of their boys, asked me how he should move forward.

"Decide what story you want to tell," was my best advice. I told Sam that though his boys were young, they would eventually ask him the same question I asked my dad: "Why did you and mom get divorced?"

Looking forward to the future and the story we want to tell might be the superpower of Enneagram Threes because of our future orientation to time. The future will happen. And we can help people, perhaps people who live too much in the present, to remember the future.

It sounds strange to remember events that haven't happened yet, but when others are consumed with their pasts or what's happening right now, the gift we give echoes the wisdom my mother taught me about life: this too shall pass. Life, faith, and growth all lie ahead of us, which prompts us to move past the emotions and sensations of the day or moment to envision the life we want for ourselves and for the people we love.

> Today, look for and notice the opportunities when your orientation to the future is genuinely helpful to others. Trust that a future orientation to time does not always pull you out of the moment but pulls others into seeing and living a desired future. How you see future moments is a blessing to those around you. They need you to help them see that this too shall pass.

RELEASING THE FALSE

FR. RICHARD ROHR WRITES, "Our first experience of life is primarily felt in the body. . . . We know ourselves in the security of those who hold us and gaze upon us. It's not heard or seen or thought, it's felt. That's the original knowing."

We are shaped first and most deeply by our primarily caretakers. Parents, grandparents, siblings, or foster care workers may have offered messages that caused Threes to learn to repress their feelings.

During my first trip to see John, my therapist, he asked me, "How do you *feel* about that?"

He might as well have asked me about quantum physics or cold fusion. I understood the question from having heard others talk about their feelings, but I could not identify them. John began naming feelings: sadness, happiness, joy, and so on. I wanted to know, in discrete detail, which feeling was which, and I just couldn't get there. I was blank.

I felt joy and fear when my daughters were born. I cried endless tears when Rochelle and I were married (though I lied to my parents about the pollen or some other allergen that was in no way active in the thick January winter). I laugh. In fact, I love to laugh. It's my favorite. But those deep feelings that others felt seemed to elude me.

I'd spent so much of my life pushing aside feelings or outright ignoring them that, like an equation learned in high school chemistry, I recognized the factors but had no ability to work them out. I had to rediscover what feeling was—at least feelings other than anger and shame, which had never abandoned me.

Months after my first session with John, I was reminded of part of the Jewish Shema: "love Him, your True God, with all your heart and soul, with every ounce of your strength" (Deuteronomy 6:5). For centuries, Judaism has invited humanity to love God with the mind, which is where feelings flow from. After all, our *feelings* about life and our circumstances grow out of what we *think* about them. Our thoughts can change our feelings.

The same mental and intellectual focus that Threes bring to projects and systems can be rerouted to focus on our feelings as well, but that won't happen by accident. I have to choose to feel. I have to examine what I'm feeling when my instinct is to ignore it. All this means slowing down, noticing, and allowing feelings to arouse themselves. It means dealing with feelings when they awaken and pausing to notice and allow them. It means naming feelings for what they are rather than what I want them to be. Experiencing feelings is a kind of discipline, complete with all the intention and suffering that comes with forming a new discipline. Feeling feelings, then, becomes like training for a marathon: little by little, over time, taking one step, then another, then another.

What's most important for me though, at least today, is not feeling but the *choice* to feel. Each of us is born into a family, social, religious, and relational system without being consulted about our gifts and deficits, but children do grow up. The apostle Paul writes that as a child he thought as a child, but the day came when he put childish things away. For Enneagram Threes maturity means embracing all aspects of being human, especially our feelings.

What might happen today if you decided to choose to feel?

WHO CARES?

"DO YOU THINK people care about the way I feel?"

When I asked the question, John, my therapist, looked at me like I had asked which clouds are easiest to walk on.

And when people asked about what I was feeling or how I was feeling, I struggled to answer honestly, because I thought people didn't care. Not really.

After lots of Enneagram work, reality hit me. I rarely shared how I was feeling, because I didn't really care how other people were feeling. There were a few times, sensing that something meaningful and deep was happening, that I asked the people I cared about how they were feeling. And there were times I genuinely cared—but not many.

I push through life conquering, and feelings aren't conquerable. Feelings force me to stop, ask, ponder, and delve. I get irked when people slow my momentum with emotions that I can't do anything about.

Since Enneagram Threes aren't inclined to hear other people's deeper and more complex feelings, we assume they aren't interested in hearing about ours. We're attuned to others' feelings that are helpful for us to meet our goals but often not much more. We are so concerned about getting things done that we simply ignore our feelings and inner world, but by ignoring our inner world we abandon our very selves.

The ancient Hebrews routinely expressed their emotions to one another and God. It's easy to believe that people and God are primarily or perhaps only interested in hearing about my highlight reel, but they are not. The Scriptures reveal emotions that are unpolished and real. Emotions and experiences chronicled in verses like Psalm 88:3: "My soul is deeply troubled, and *my heart can't bear the weight of this sorrow.* I feel so close to death." The Psalms shatter my illusions that God's interest in my life is limited to my triumphs. For ancient Israel, the Psalms were their playlist of joy, celebration, lament, anger, and even irritation with God. There are sentiments in the Psalms that get strained out in the typical Bible class. But there they are, all the same.

The Psalms give me emotional freedom. The Psalms are unvarnished. Anger, joy, disappointment, and disillusionment rip through nearly every page. And through it all, God still loves the singers and pray-ers of the Psalms. Emotional honesty, it turns out, is not disqualifying. Far from it.

In the Psalms I find freedom in the knowledge that what I feel, regardless of how hard it is for me to name, is real and valid and worthy of being voiced. Where Threes have learned to curate and guard our most intimate feelings, the

Psalms grant us freedom to liberate our hidden emotions. I can name my experience through my emotions, and those who love me best will draw closer rather than move farther away. Like all good parents, God longs for honest communication about our lived experiences. God cares about the way I feel and about the way you feel. And if God can do that, maybe the people God brings into our lives, the people who live with us and walk alongside us, care about our feelings too.

Today may be the perfect opportunity to be honest with yourself, with God, and with the people who love you. Maybe today is the day you let other people care about how you feel.

ALL WILL BE WELL

ENNEAGRAM THREES TAKE IN DATA from the world by feeling what other people are feeling, as long as they don't go too deep or become inefficient. We have a sense of what the room wants and needs. We feel the temperature in the room. Yet while we know what other people feel, we don't explore our own feelings when navigating the world or making decisions.

We feel everything yet believe how *we* feel doesn't matter. We believe how other people feel matters, especially their feelings about whether or not they like, esteem, or admire us. Add all that together and you get a population of folks who always feel responsible. This responsibility isn't associated with being needed or necessary but is a sense of responsibility that those around us have a valuable experience and get what they need. That's how Threes become people-pleasers and performers.

For instance, years ago my teacher, Suzanne Stabile, was leading a workshop at my church. She and her husband, Joe, traveled to Houston the night before Suzanne was to teach, but no one on our staff team who invited Suzanne had taken the extra step and invited her and Joe for dinner or offered any other generosities of hospitality. I was appalled! Would Suzanne think our church was a den of inhospitality, filled with uncaring people? I invited them to our home, and we had a great night sharing and laughing together. When the weekend was over, I felt like I had rescued the entire event. Suzanne and Joe certainly could have managed dinner in a city with the most diverse food selection in the country, but I wanted them to have a great time. I felt responsible not because of my feelings but because of theirs.

What happened that night wasn't about dinner; it was about my Triad and Stance. My desire for someone to feel welcomed meant I had to *do* something (Aggressive Stance). We do things for the sake of other people's feelings about us, whether or not we feel like it or it makes sense. What often is lost is that we achieve and succeed for the sake of relationships.

All that can become exhausting. Doing for the sake of others doesn't stop with dinners but extends itself into over-functioning on work teams, attempts to control outcomes— even over events which aren't terribly important—and seeing even the innocuous and everyday occurrences as problems to be solved.

Left unchecked, Threes can fool themselves into believing that responsibilities lay on their doorstep when they actually don't. The world is not ours to save. It's okay to keep a keen eye out for the work designed for you to do and the work that *only* you can do.

Today, when you feel prompted to do something because you fear the loss of esteem from others if you don't do it, try *not* doing what you're tempted to do. Practice not doing anything. See what happens. Most people carry with them an invisible bucket of tasks that they would love for someone to take off their hands. Take note of who is still there to help, and you'll discover that all that feeling and doing were never expected of you.

FOLLOW THE PATH

FROM THE TIME I WAS TWELVE until I was twenty, I never cried. I decided to be steel. Unmoved. Impenetrable. As it turns out, though, not even Vulcans can remain emotionless forever. Eventually the dam breaks and the tears flow. These days I'm often surprised by when and where I find myself leaky-eyed.

I once served on the advisory board for my alma mater, Abilene Christian University, but we didn't do much advising. We heard stories about events at the school. We voted on a couple of post-graduate scholarships for exceptional students and spent weekends being the first to hear about upgrades to the campus facilities. But one update brought me to tears. And of all things, it was an update about a running trail.

At the end of a long weekend of cold cut lunches and rubber chicken dinners, the chief architect—who had to have a more official title than "chief architect"—presented a report about the new running trail surrounding the school. He shared about a new grove of trees being planted and the lighting scheme created to provide maximum visibility for nighttime runners. He talked about how his team had to choose between a trail made of recycled rubber, which was supposed to be better for runners' feet and knees, and the much less expensive concrete option. As he told us, a large state school chose the rubber option. He drove four hours to their campus, sat on a bench all afternoon, and noticed that no runners—neither students nor teachers—ran on the rubber track. They all ran on the street, so he decided to go with cheaper concrete over the unused and more expensive recycled rubber.

In the midst of this routine report, he paused. "What we do," he said, "is not nearly as important as why we do it. College is stressful, and running is a great stress reducer. Maybe students are away from home for the first time or experiencing loneliness. Maybe they are on a walk with their boyfriend or girlfriend or a girl they are working up the courage to ask on a date. Some students on the trail will be breaking up, and they are nervous and scared. Other students are trying to take control of their lives, their fitness, and are getting in shape for the first time. Still others may find in a walk around campus the ready-made remedy for a difficult roommate. Life decisions will be made on that track."

The humanity he saw in our students broke me open. Tears. I'm in tears now thinking about it. In that moment, I heard a man who knew *why* he worked. It made me think of a quote some attribute to Pablo Picasso: "The meaning of life is to find your gift. The purpose of life is to give it away."

Thousands of students won't ever know the name of the man behind their track, but every day he thinks about them. Fulfillment, for him, wasn't in acknowledgment or adulation. His success will never be noticed or noted by the thousands of students who do on the trail exactly what he envisioned they would do. They will only know their lives were changed on a concrete trail that someone planned and built while never thinking about the one who planned and built it.

Creator God, deepen in me a motivation to serve others without regard for praise and, in fact, in search of anonymity. Help me find the beauty in offering my gifts as a service to the world, trusting that in doing so, I will be seen wholly and completely, even if only by you. Amen.

CRIPPLED LAMBS, CRIPPLED LEADERS

Leadership lands on the doorstep of Enneagram Threes. I've been leading things since junior T-ball. Threes' positivity, energy, and the competency we project give others the sense that we're up for any task, but that may not be a good thing.

Leader is not a synonym of whole, good, complete, or healthy. Here's what I mean: people are obsessed with leadership—leadership training, leadership conferences, leadership retreats, and leadership books. I recently read an article warning me about parenting behaviors that were potentially crippling children from "becoming leaders." Since I don't want my children to be "crippled," as the article suggested, I guessed I'd better get my rear in gear and make sure my two curly haired daughters aren't incapacitated for life. What if they don't grow up to be leaders?

The world needs good leaders, for sure. The problem is being overly focused on borrowed-from-the-boardroom, bigger, slicker, shinier leadership, supported by an orgy of leadership products that have made leadership itself the goal. What's more, this can be dangerous for Enneagram Threes, who are too often made leaders even when we shouldn't be. Allowing the culture to force leadership upon us will only drive Threes deeper into the dysfunctions of our number.

The leaders I most admire found their way to crosses, prisons, lions' dens, Roman courts, exile, or suffered an assassin's knife or gun—not onto the bestseller lists, or into the C-Suite or CEO's office. The greatest leaders' ears are filled with the complaints and criticisms of the people they are called to lead, not the applause of stadiums or throngs of eager enthusiasts waiting hours deep in lines at book signings. While I do not begrudge anyone their book signings, shouldn't it give us pause when the lives of modern leaders look so starkly different from the leaders we most esteem? Speaking of his own faith tradition, Henri Nouwen wrote, "The way of the Christian leader is not the way of upward mobility in which our world has invested so much, but the way of downward mobility ending on the cross."

Scripture gives us little indication that Jesus' disciple Judas was a bad guy—up until he betrays Jesus. Judas was a leader and was on the inside. His motivation for trading Jesus for thirty pieces of silver, some scholars suggest, was a simple attempt to jump-start what he felt was a stalled revolution. With swords finally drawn, Jesus would have to get on with kingdom building and quit hanging out with prostitutes and people with leprosy. It's not that Judas was against sinners; they just weren't useful in the grand scheme. The insurgency wasn't happening quickly enough, so Judas decided to step up and be a leader.

Jesus, on the other hand, wasn't about leadership—not as we define it. He wasn't even about "servant-leadership." Jesus was about sacrifice. He gave up his seat, released his platform, silenced his voice, and relinquished his power. Jesus did not leverage his leadership. He surrendered it!

> What would it look like for you to lead by sacrifice? To allow others to win the day; to speak last; to give your influence away? Think about this the next time you're leading something: the leaders who changed the world ended up battered and bruised.

THE ANTIDOTE TO SHAME

THERE ARE SOME PEOPLE you can tell almost anything to, because whatever story you share, they have a similar version. Elaine is often that for me. She and I share the same interest in sports, theology, writing, and public speaking. We also share the same Enneagram number, and something about our confluence of similarities makes our conversations a kind of confession. Most of those confessions are about our bodies, our image.

After losing one hundred pounds in 2014, in six years I added back ten pounds, which is understandable for a man my age. I still lift weights, cross-train, run, and cycle. There's little my body can't do, but the weight I added back is in the last place I want it, and some days it takes all I have to leave the house. Still, looking at pictures of myself at my lowest weight makes me queasy. I felt like a failure—a loser, quite frankly.

Enneagram Threes are in the Feeling Triad where a dominant emotion is shame—a profound feeling that we are so inherently flawed that we are unworthy of love. And the first thing shame does is isolate us. It ignites our fight-or-flight response, typically forcing us into fighting our battles alone and running away from others. In the end, all the energy and optimism natural for Threes gets wasted in isolation. Curt Thompson captures our plight in *The Soul of Shame*:

> When we experience shame, we tend to turn away from others because the prospect of being seen or known by another carries the anticipation of shame being intensified or reactivated. However, the very act of turning away, while temporarily protecting and relieving us from our feeling (and the gaze of the "other"), ironically simultaneously reinforces the very shame we are attempting to avoid.

Since shame turns us inward on ourselves and away from others, the remedy is sharing in community. Once we take the lionhearted step to be vulnerable, storytelling opens space for truthfulness and decreases the availability for deceit.

Healing requires rejecting shame's most potent weapon: isolation. That means finding someone to share your story with—the whole unaltered, unedited version—and then finding a community to share your story with. You will discover that everyone else has a shame story too.

Write down the names of two or three people you can trust. Make a plan to contact them today, and when you get together, share one or two aspects of your current life that you might be tempted to shade over. This is a path to healing!

SITTING AROUND

THERE'S A CHAIR IN MY home study that is reserved for sitting. Aren't all chairs for sitting, you ask? Well, this is for a special kind of sitting. Every Monday I force myself to just sit. No reading. No writing. No sliding through articles on my iPad or playing games. I just sit.

It's not as spiritual as it sounds. I'm not doing contemplative prayer. I'm not working my way through an Ignatian Examen, connecting with the universe, or the hundred other centering practices that are available. I just sit. Sometimes I look out the window.

I sit for the solitude.

Solitude invites us to deal with ourselves. It is like getting dressed without a mirror, which is not as horrible as it sounds. Solitude frees me from my personality's demand to be centered on people and the esteem that comes from delighting them. And that feels lonely.

I spend my energy on other people, trying to gain their affirmation and validation at the expense of my inner self and feelings. When there is no one to react to, there is no one to affirm me. When I sit in solitude, the writing projects, product launches, and other tasks can't and won't be celebrated. Philosopher Dallas Willard wrote, "Solitude well practiced will break the power of busyness, haste, isolation, and loneliness. You will see that the world is not on your shoulders after all. Your will find yourself." And every week I discover that I am a person worth knowing.

You too, are a person worth knowing, but knowing yourself begins by doing something few people every suspect is necessary: getting to know yourself.

I bought my wife tickets to a reading by one of her favorite authors one Mother's Day. I added a hefty wad of cash and a new journal, and encouraged her to take the entire day to do what she wished. he did something that I would have never thought of, but it launched a practice that I have embraced. She made a list of things in her journal she likes—books, music, people, food, everything.

Before that, I never really thought about what I liked. But I discover more of what I like and who I am in my chair on Mondays. It's an act of will to convince myself that I'm not wasting time or burning hours, but each week I know more than I knew the previous week. I know myself.

Ruminate on what gives you life. When your mind starts to wander, forgive yourself and come back, asking yourself what you love and examining the times you've felt most free and alive. Rediscover yourself.

OUR PRACTICE

YEARS AGO I STARTED practicing yoga. I didn't call it a practice at the time because I didn't know what to call it. As part of a fitness program, one day each week was dedicated to yoga, just thirty minutes. I hated it. I exercised to lose fat and gain muscle. Running five miles felt right and so did lifting weights. Even on hard days, I could see the connection between my work and my goals. I didn't feel that way on yoga days. Doing yoga, I would barely break a sweat. I knew from my other workouts that transformation takes time, but even after a couple of years in, yoga was going nowhere and it left me feeling empty and worried that I had wasted my time.

If the definition of insanity is doing the same thing over and over again, but expecting different results, then I was in trouble. My incredibly tight hamstrings remained incredibly tight. My heels never quite touched the floor in downward dog, and all the while I would be flexible one week and rigid the next. But this was yoga. Millions of people over thousands of years have practiced yoga. Were they all crazy?

I was doing the same thing over and over expecting a different result, but only because my expectations were wrong. Once, while rolling my eyes through yet another Vinyasa, my instructor mentioned "our practice." He said our practice was about finding inner calm, a kind of peace that connects our spirit to our body in a world that dissociates the two. He was right. I had dissociated my inner being from my body, and the daily stress and anxiety I experienced was evidence of it.

I began yoga hoping to make my body better, more flexible, and resistant to injury, but I was heading in the wrong direction. That's what an unwavering focus on destination over presence does. It focuses our attention on the journey's end, shrouding us from the unmistakable beauties and warnings present to us. I found that truth in my yoga "insanity."

Yoga is a profound practice of presence. There are countless free yoga practices available on streaming services like YouTube. Find one. Dedicate yourself to a few days of yoga using a simple breath prayer. Breathe in, "I am a child of God." Breathe out, "This is the only place I need to be."

WHAT'S MOST IMPORTANT?

IS THERE SOMEONE you know who reminds you of yourself? The self you don't want to be?

For me it was David. There was a kind of florescence in his eyes that wanted to give off light, but it diffused and gave everything a yellowish glow. It wasn't sunlight. He once told me about growth at his church, young families coming in droves. He mentioned how well his kids were flourishing and how well he and his wife were doing, but I knew it wasn't true. And he knew I knew he was lying. David is an unhealthy Enneagram Three.

When you've decided that your worth is in accomplishment, failure feels like worthlessness. No matter who or how many people tell you otherwise, once earning your worth settles into your bones, there are not many remedies.

In so many ways I had been and am like him, and seeing him forced me to confront the me I do not like. When I saw him, I saw the unhealthiest parts of me, and perhaps that's why I reacted so strongly. It might be argued that Threes are less concerned with success and more compelled by a fear of failure and a loss of worth. And I had a good dose of judgmentalism to throw in as well.

Seeing myself in David prompted me to ask hard questions about my own worth and value. For the first time I didn't just ponder whether or not I wanted to be successful. I asked a deeper question: In which areas of life is it *most* important for me to be successful? For me, this was more than the stereotypical "winning at work and at home" proposition. And so I had to choose which aspects of life were more important, and allow other aspects to be "good enough."

To choose what matters most I have to allocate resources, realizing that there is not enough time, money, energy, or focus to be everything to everyone and be a full and whole-hearted person. The power and beauty are in the choosing rather than the striving.

Imagine a life where we get to choose our successes (and mediocrities). Where we allow our innermost being to determine when to start and when to stop, when to rest and breathe, and when to engage or let it go. Imagine a world where what is most important gets treated like it's most important. Maybe then, when someone asks how life is going, we can share authentic light.

Examine your thoughts and feelings about people you perceive as failures. Does failure entice you to move toward or away from others? Reflect on what it is you fear about failure.

THE FAR SIDE OF FAILURE

YOU ARE NOT STATIC. No one is. We all shift and adapt to our surroundings and our immediate needs. Enneagram wisdom recognizes we are not simply one way, working from one set of motivations all the time. With different people or in different seasons of life, our core fears and compulsions shift. This is especially true in times of stress and emotional security. Each number needs the behaviors of their stress and security numbers to maneuver through life's dynamic changes. Thus, experiencing failure is the way we find security.

Beginning in 2004, I experienced a season of profound and public failures. It started when the senior pastor at the church I served moved away and I began preaching most weeks in the interim. Soon church members began asking, "Why are we looking for a new senior pastor when Sean is right here. Let's just hire him." And then they asked me, "Sean, do you want the job?" And I listened to them, not realizing the people doing the asking weren't the same people doing the hiring.

I went ahead and put my hat in the ring, and it came down to me and one other candidate, and I didn't get the job. Turns out, the church leadership thought I was too young and inexperienced.

For Threes there are two events which feel like death: failure and embarrassment. I had failed and was embarrassed. And it wasn't just in my head. People in our denomination made jokes about me. *How good could you be if your own church, the people who know you, won't hire you?* constantly rang in my head. There was a deep sense of shame. It was the first time in my life that I had ever failed at anything, and I failed spectacularly and publicly.

A few years after this very public crash-and-burn, two church leaders walked into my office and told me I was fired. They didn't do it in the normal churchy way. In the church world, we have a lot of different language for fired. "We're making a transition. We're being led in another direction. This is a season of pruning." I didn't hear any of those. I got fired. This was death on top of death.

"Can we do this in a way that my children don't have to find out that dad was fired?" I asked. I didn't think I could live with that. They agreed. We kept it our little secret. When the girls were older, I told the whole tale, but at the time, it would've felt like a mortal wound.

It wasn't long after that I thought I'd found a great escape. I had been talking with a church in Northern California. So, we took that job and moved outside of San Francisco, but there was conflict, not *from* day one, but *before* day one.

So after three years of stress and disappointment, I was nearly done with ministry. Three years later my family returned to Texas to work with a small church near my mother-in-law, and I was convinced that within a few years, I'd be selling insurance. But things changed. That church was amazing to and for our family. I began to write and speak more. I discovered that there was purpose in my work and a path forward.

There was a revelation on the far side of failure of who my friends were—who loved me, and what to be loyal to. Too much of life is spent believing that commitments should be made to positive outcomes. In the process, people sometimes get run over or left behind. Failure taught me that my competencies, or lack thereof, were not truly me. Today I write, speak across the country, coach speakers, and serve a large, dynamic church, none of which defines me, because I am the same person I was when no person of influence wanted to be in my zip code.

In times of inner surety or release, Enneagram Threes begin to connect more deeply with other people. Life become less about individual achievement and more about collaboration. True friends, those who want relationships with us and not merely to use our gifts, skills, and energy for their own ends, are unearthed.

One of the best ways to experience security is accepting failure as failure rather than following the self-deceptive path of flippantly reframing failure. In failure is the opportunity to know real friends.

> **Ask yourself: What do I truly fear losing if I fail or am perceived as a failure? Who will I lose?**

FIND A HOBBY

"NO ONE EVER GOT TO THE END of their life wishing they'd spent more time at work," the saying goes. But the saying is nonsense. Plenty of people reach the end of their days wishing that they had worked more or harder. We just say it differently. We say, "I wish I had written that book." "I regret not being able to take my wife to Paris or saddling my kids with college debt." It can also sound like, "I can't afford to keep the house." Lots of people reach their final days wishing, but not saying, they had worked more or produced more or earned more.

But that's not the way for Threes.

The Enneagram Threes I know often struggle with working *too* much. I know I do. Overwork isn't unique to Threes, but it is exceedingly common. And often not for anything as virtuous as our kid's college fund or family vacations. I work too much because I often don't know what else to do.

Some of us say, "My work is my hobby." Telling me your work is your hobby is the surest way for me to never invite you to a party. Overworking Threes can be marvelously boring. Anyway, I'm so consumed with my work, I have no interest in your work unless your work can help my work. I'm not proud of that fact—it just is.

Imagine my shock when my youngest daughter, after I scoffed at her for spending too many hours binging *The Disney Channel*, said, "Not all of us want to work all the time." She wasn't defending her actions. She was criticizing mine.

Part of the acreage that comes with the soil of a Three are the raw materials for workaholism. It's part of the temptation to find worth in production. *Just keep producing and you'll keep being worthy,* I tell myself. *People will love you if you just keep the well flowing.* And we have good reason to produce. Production allows us to pay for clothes, tuition, homes, cars, and other necessities, but the truth is that plenty of other people are able to meet all those same commitments without schlepping work home at night, carting projects along on vacation, and spending chunks of each Saturday peering into a monitor.

My friends have hobbies—photography, tennis, music. Every time I start a hobby it takes about three hours before I start scheming about how to turn it into a reputation-advancing or moneymaking venture. I say that working out is my hobby, but it's more of an unhealthy relationship with my health. I've even thought about starting a hobby so I can be the kind of person who has a hobby and fit in with people who have hobbies. It's an unhealthy motivation toward a healthy end. Life is more than work, the performance.

A mature life is more than work—it is also developing all of what brings life, a rhythm of enjoyment. A better you may be on the other side of finding new joy, learning to have fun, and appreciating relaxation.

> Maybe you should find a hobby. I can't think of a woman or man I admire who did not eventually outgrow the confines of seeing life as work on top of work and lying about the virtues of their work obsession. Pick something that you've always wanted to try, and get to work on it.

AN INVITATION
TO REST

THE WRITERS I ADMIRE MOST force themselves to sit down and write. Many do this either early in the morning or late at night, listening to the same playlist and forcing themselves to hunt and peck out a minimum word count each day. Since I wanted to write as well as they did and be as successful as they were, I adopted their habits. My day starts at 5:00 a.m. and it doesn't stop until I collapse into sleep on the couch, usually with some kind of work in my hands.

It's easy to believe our deeply held and unquestionable cultural narrative: work produces blessing. We're not entirely wrong for believing so. Yet how much of your time, energy, talent, and sweat have been spent constructing a life you can't enjoy? Are you missing the joy of your family because in the smiles of your children you see estimated payments for braces, and in their growth spurts you see clothes that barely last a season, and in the landmarks of their lives you see encroaching college tuitions? Is your response to the natural occasions of life to seek blessing from digging deeper, working longer, and constructing more?

I have discovered the antidote to overwork is sabbath. The concept of sabbath rest makes its first appearance not as a command but as God's response to God's own creativity. Sabbath does not exist as a hedge against human temptations nor a reply to a human request. It is birthed from the very life-giving rhythm of God.

After creating the cosmos, God rested. By resting, God enjoys the fruit of God's labor, celebrates the goodness which exists, trusts in the goodness of creation, and most importantly, enjoys creation for the masterpiece it is. Dorothy Bass writes, "God declares as fully possible just how very good creation is. Resting, God takes pleasure in what has been made; God has no regrets, no need to go on to create a still better world or creature more wonderful than the man and woman. In the day of rest, God's free love toward humanity takes form as time shared with them."

To put it simply: God has no need to *keep on working*!

Is there more God could have done? Of course. Could knees or eyes function better? Probably. Do annoyances like ants or cockroaches need to exist? Not for me. Could chocolate be as healthy as kale? Certainly. God pronounces creation as "good," not perfect. God's infinite power could have done infinitely more, but God's creative prerogative has never been merely to create. God desires to enjoy, and to enjoy us.

Sabbath means the most worthwhile endeavors eventually reach the point of being "enough." In Sabbath, we are freed both from working and from working on ourselves. Work will never be finished, but in six days of work it can certainly be good.

> Take a sabbath rest this week. Take time to set aside your phone, computer, and tasks to enjoy the beauty of the world and the people around you. The world will keep spinning just fine without you. That's the point of sabbath.

DISPOSABLE

I SPENT THE FIRST TWELVE YEARS of ministry as a youth pastor, which means I threw a lot of youth group parties. The most memorable was a Christmas party that I knew I was going to be late for.

I prepared and got everything ready—finding hosts, ordering food, making invites; I even gave my volunteers a minute-by-minute schedule. The kids and volunteers thought my down-to-the-minute schedule was strange. Who plans a party down to the minute? they asked.

Arriving late to the party, I found that stranger things than my schedule were afoot. Our host had served pizza on plastic, disposable plates and after dinner had the kids stack the plates next to the sink so she could wash them. I had never seen someone wash disposable plates. (The intended use of disposable plates is to dispose of them—maybe to recycle them, but not to wash them.) If I had wanted to wash dishes, I would have used real dishes. Yet the stack of pizza-stained plastic dishes sitting a mile high next to the sink birthed a question in me: What am I holding on to that I should let go?

The word that came back to me and continues to haunt me is *comparison*.

But Threes aren't simply competitors, we are constant comparers.

Who's up? Who's down? Who's ahead? Who's behind? All of these occupy my mind at least part of the day, but the nagging obsession is whether others are up, down, ahead of, or behind *me*. How do I compare? How do I stack up?

Like disposable plastic, that mode of living has to be released. If we tell ourselves that we are up and ahead of others because of our own ingenuity and industry, we cannot help but carry the arrogance that accompanies those thoughts. On the other hand, if we tell ourselves we're down and behind others, it feels like losing a game we refuse to admit we're playing.

Constant comparison trains us to hold on to what was intended to be disposable—jealousies, anger about real or perceived slights, suspicions of worthlessness, the false belief that we are inherently flawed. Comparison is corrosive. It feeds us into a loop of considering who or what is "up" or "down" and where we and others fit. Comparison lies by insinuating that life isn't dynamic by suggesting that if we were worthwhile we'd always be up and never down.

Comparison exterminates our hope for contentment. Who can be content when there's a race to run, a colleague to best, a friend to outpace? Comparison makes it impossible to be happy for two groups of people: you, and everyone else.

The only countermeasure to comparison is gratitude. Comparison thrives in me by magnifying the gaps in life: what's not as I think or was told it should be, or my lack of accomplishments. Gratitude highlights the places life has been and is being made whole. Comparison sees the house renovations I can't yet afford, which my friends can. Gratitude sees a house that shelters and a home that loves. Comparison sees muscles unformed. Gratitude hears the heart that pumps life.

Today is the day for letting go. As the Buddhist saying reminds us: "Letting go gives freedom, and freedom is the only condition for happiness."

What can you let go of today? A perceived slight? A simmering resentment? An argument? What comparison is dragging you down? How can you let it go today?

YOUR INHERENT VIRTUES

THERE ARE PEOPLE WHO BENEFIT from your unconscious compulsions, which are those times you're living in *excess* in your number. When you're living in excess in your number, it's as if your normal motivations and behaviors get a steroid shot. You're more focused and more productive.

When I began to get serious about my physical fitness, most everyone I knew was supportive. The kudos and congratulations were daily and encouraging. Then they stopped. Somewhere I hit an inflection point when the celebration ended and the criticism began. "Aren't you taking this a little too seriously? When will it end?" Polite questioning wasn't the end, though. The next phase of the critique was temptation. "Of course, you can have some pie; you eat too healthy. Skip your workout and come have beers with us. It's just one day." After that came shame and disconnection. "I don't enjoy having lunch with you. I feel gross and unhealthy."

I was shaken by how personally I felt these miniature reproofs. More than being shaken, I was surprised. I thought getting healthy was always something to celebrate, and then

I realized that not everyone wanted me to be healthy. My drive, optimism, self-assurance, and work ethic are good for people but turned southward can become negatives for me and those closest to me. It's true for all of us. So, what happens when we decide to get healthy? People love it—until they don't.

The great temptation to finding your healing, moving past your number, and entering into your essence (who you were created to be) is just not quitting. You've started. Don't quit. There will be pitfalls. Other people are not used to you being less focused on their emotional needs. Colleagues are not accustomed to finishing their pieces of the task without you. People rest easy under the assurance that you have a plan. These are gifts Threes offer the world, but they are not gifts we have to offer all the time. You will be tempted to regress to the norm, to return to the exile from which you have desperately sought to be freed. There will be plenty of people ready for you to return to their expectations of you. Their aspirations for you are not your concern. Freedom means releasing ourselves from the tyranny of other people's expectations. It may take a while for folks to clue in, buy in, and figure it out, but expectations are a ruse keeping others from experiencing the real you—the you as you were meant to be.

God, show me the places where I am moving backward into the comfortable and expected. Reveal to me the spaces inside where my compulsions are serving others but not serving me. Give me wisdom to embrace the changes you are bringing to me. Amen.

THE SEA IS NEVER FULL

"ECCLESIASTES IS GOD'S BULLDOZER," my friend Mike says. Ecclesiastes sounds a different tone than most books of the Bible. When we might well expect uplift, encouragement, or comfort, at some points Ecclesiastes gives us what seems like discouragement:

> What good does it do anyone to work so hard *again and again*,
> sun up to sundown? *All his labor to gain but a little?*
> One generation comes, another goes;
> but the earth continues to remain.
> The sun rises and the sun sets,
> laboring to come up quickly to its place again *and again*.
> The wind in its travels blows toward the south,
> then swings back around to the north.
> Back and forth,
> returning in its circuit again *and again*.
> All rivers flow to the sea,
> but the sea is never full. (Ecclesiastes 1:3-7)

It's hard to miss the implication that life is a meaningless, purposeless wheel that we spin on until our hearts or lungs give out or some disease wrestles us to the floor. We're born, we go to school, go to work, have kids, retire . . . and then die. It's not that you're not special; it's just that your life is not unique. And guess what happens the day after you die? The sun comes up again.

Imagine my surprise when I was asked to attend a youth camp one summer and speak about Ecclesiastes. This is just what teenagers want to hear. "Here ya go, kids. In the middle of your puberty, discovering yourself, and looking forward to life's endless possibilities, you should know only your momma thinks you're special and life is a beatdown. Now, go live your dreams." Abolitionist Harriet Beecher Stowe said, "Never give up, for that is the place and time that the tide will turn." Ecclesiastes seems closer to, "Go ahead. Give up!"

Preparing for summer camp, I had a lot of work to do, and most of that work was inside of me. Searching through the Bible, my soul, and my life, I excavated a gem from this seeming cave of desolation. Ecclesiastes was inviting me out of my personality, out of my attempts to be noticed and my power-grabbing. The perennial struggle for Enneagram Threes is the desire to be noticed. The temptation never goes away, and resisting it calls for our hypervigilance. Ecclesiastes showed me that all my attempts to be the center—which are actually attempts to be loved—were misguided. I was deploying tactics that could not possibly deliver what I craved. In life, we will never be pretty enough or smart enough or successful enough to soothe what really aches. We will never get enough acknowledgment or kudos to fill up that place inside us.

"All streams flow to the sea, but the sea is never full," says the Teacher in Ecclesiastes.

The sea never gets full enough. That's why after years of work Enneagram Threes still find it tempting to give people their résumés. It's why we struggle to sit still and are always busy with new projects. It's why we feel bitter when slighted, why we get angry when someone else gets credit for our work, why offense comes so easily, and why jealousy percolates when seeing the lives of people who seem to be doing better than us. *Our sea is never full.*

If the wisdom of Ecclesiastes is true, and chasing triumph after triumph is ultimately meaningless, what is the best way to spend what Mary Oliver calls "your one wild and precious life"? Ecclesiastes knows the answer:

So *here is what you should do:* go and enjoy your meals, drink your wine and love *every minute of* it because God is already pleased with what you do. Dress your best, and don't forget a splash of scented fragrance. Enjoy life with the woman you love. Cherish every moment of the fleeting life which God has given you under the sun. For this is your lot in life, *your great reward* for all of your hard work under the sun. Whatever you find to do, do it well because where you are going—the grave—there will be no working or thinking or knowing or wisdom. (Ecclesiastes 9:7-10)

While there will always be work, there is no need for endless striving. There is no need for obsession. Life is not given for the sake of achievement. It is given for the sake of love. Love every minute of it.

> Make a list of everything you love about yourself. Keep it somewhere near you at all times—a wallet, purse, or as a note on your phone. When you feel the ache of not being enough, the pull to do more or be more, check back through your list and remind yourself: you are loveable, and you are loved.

NOTES

6   *Why are you always giving*: Rob Reiner, *A Few Good Men* (Castle Rock Entertainment, Columbia Pictures, 1992).

8   *The world tells you many lies*: Henri J. M. Nouwen, *Life of the Beloved: Spiritual Living in a Secular World* (London: Hodder Stoughton, 1992).

17   *The glory of God*: St. Irenaeus of Lyon, *Against Heresies*, vol. 4 (Lyon, AD 180), 20:7.

19   *The ego hates losing*: Richard Rohr, *Falling Upward: A Spirituality for the Two Halves of Life* (San Francisco: Jossey-Bass, 2011), 47.

24   *For as long as you can*: Henri Nouwen, *The Inner Voice of Love: A Journey Through Anguish to Freedom* (New York: Image, 1999), 5.

28   *training for reigning*: Dallas Willard's written teaching on this topic can be found in chapter nine of *The Divine Conspiracy (*San Francisco: Harper, 1998), but this exact wording is not in the text.

37   *deceit what it is*: Don Richard Riso and Russ Hudson, *Understanding the Enneagram: The Practical Guide to Personality Types* (New York: Mariner Books, 2000), 43.

40   *But the older I get*: Thanks to my friend Dr. Richard Beck for introducing me to the life and work St. Thérèse.

41   *I feel within me other vocations*: St. Thérèse of Lisiuex, *The Story of a Soul: The Autobiography of the Little Flower* (Charlotte, NC: Tan Books, 2010), 192.

41   *I finally had rest*: St. Thérèse of Lisiuex, *The Story of a Soul*, 194.

49   *Envy works best*: William H. Willimon, *Sinning Like a Christian: A New Look at the 7 Deadly Sins* (Nashville: Abingdon Press, 2013), 44.

52   *There is perhaps only one*: Paul Kalanithi, *When Breath Becomes Air* (New York: Random House, 2016), 199.

65   *The Five Lies of Identity*: Henri Nouwen, *Who Are We? Henri Nouwen on Our Christian Identity*. Narrated by Henri Nouwen. Audible, 2017. Audiobook.

66 *We are not what we do*: Henri Nouwen, *Home Tonight: Further Reflections on the Parable of the Prodigal Son* (New York: Doubleday, 2009), 38-39.

77 *Stress is for*: National Broadcasting Company (February 6, 2002), "Night Five," *West Wing*, Burbank, California.

82 *Our first experience of life*: Richard Rohr, *Everything Belongs: The Gift of Contemplative Prayer* (Spring Valley, NY: Crossroad, 2003).

92 *The meaning of life*: See "The Purpose of Life Is to Discover Your Gift. The Meaning of Life Is to Give Your Gift Away" (June 16, 2014), Quote Investigator, retrieved April 23, 2020, from https://quoteinvestigator.com/2014/06/16/purpose-gift/.

95 *The way of the Christian leader*: Henri J. M. Nouwen, *In the Name of Jesus: Reflections on Christian Leadership* (Spring Valley, NY: Crossroad, 1989), 81-82.

97 *Enneagram Threes are in the Feeling*: See "How the Enneagram System Works," The Enneagram Institute, https://www.enneagraminstitute.com/how-the-enneagramw-system-works.

98 *When we experience shame*: Curt Thompson, *The Soul of Shame: Retelling the Stories We Believe About Ourselves* (Downers Grove, IL: InterVarsity Press, 2015), 31.

100 *Solitude well practiced will break*: Dallas Willard, *The Great Omission: Reclaiming Jesus's Essential Teachings on Discipleship* (New York: HarperCollins, 2006), 36.

112 *God declares as fully possible*: Dorothy Bass, *Practicing Our Faith: A Way of Life for Searching People* (Minneapolis: Fortress Press, 2019), 78.

116 *Letting go gives*: Thich Nhat Hanh, *The Heart of the Buddha's Teaching: Transforming Suffering into Peace, Joy, and Liberation* (New York: Random House, 1998), 78.

120 *Never give up*: Tracy Quinn, *Quotable Women of the Twentieth Century* (New York: W. Morrow, 1999), 219.

121 *your one wild*: Mary Oliver, *Devotions: The Selected Poems of Mary Oliver* (London: Penguin Press, 2017), 316.

ENNEAGRAM
DAILY REFLECTIONS

SUZANNE STABILE,
SERIES EDITOR